THE DIARY OF ANNE FRANK

DRAMATIZED BY
FRANCES GOODRICH
AND **ALBERT HACKETT**

(BASED UPON THE BOOK
ANNE FRANK: DIARY OF A YOUNG GIRL)

★

★

DRAMATISTS
PLAY SERVICE
INC.

THE DIARY OF ANNE FRANK was first presented by Kermit Bloomgarden at the Cort Theatre, New York City, on October 5, 1955. It was directed by Garson Kanin and the production was designed by Boris Aronson. The cast was as follows:

MR. FRANK .... Joseph Schildkraut

MIEP .... Gloria Jones

MRS. VAN DAAN .... Dennie Moore

MR. DAN DAAN .... Lou Jacobi

PETER VAN DAAN .... David Levin

MRS. FRANK .... Gusti Huber

MARGOT FRANK .... Eva Rubinstein

ANNE FRANK .... Susan Strasberg

MR. KRALER .... Clinton Sundberg

MR. DUSSEL .... Jack Gilford

THE TIME: During the years of World War II and immediately thereafter.

THE PLACE: Amsterdam.

There are two acts.

DESCRIPTION OF SET

SCENE: The scene remains the same throughout the play. The top floors of a warehouse in Amsterdam, Holland. The sharply peaked roof of the building is outlined against a sea of other rooftops, stretching away in the distance. Nearby is the belfry of a church tower, the Westertoren, whose carillon rings out the hours.

The three rooms of the top floor and a small attic space above are exposed to our view. The largest of the rooms is in the center, with two small rooms, slightly raised, on either side. The area is cramped and inhospitable. Unfinished plaster walls are cracked and crumbling, stained wallpaper is fading on some walls, and raw bricks are exposed beneath. Heavy naked beams cut through the center room.

Everyone on the stage is in view at all times. The people not in a scene move about enough to seem natural, but their movements are never fast or sudden or so unusual as to attract attention.

RIGHT ROOM

At the extreme D. R., a chaise longue, with legs removed, rests on the floor parallel to the curtain line. Its head is R. against the wall. At its foot is a low wooden box that extends the length of this bed. Immediately upstage in the R. wall, is a window and windowseat. The lid of this seat may be raised. The window is covered with a two-ply, dark brown, blackout curtain. The wall jogs toward C. at the upstage edge of the window and on this wall face are seven wooden pegs. The U. R. wall is covered with many pictures and photographs, thumbtacked in place. Queen Wilhelmina, a small map of Holland, Shirley Temple, Garbo, Robert Taylor, are in the collection. A cot has been placed along this side with its head against the rear wall. In the C. of the rear wall we see a window with dirty, frosted panes. Under the window is a low chest of drawers. The L. wall consists only of the door flat, U. L. This door has two panes of glass that have been painted over, and it is hinged on the upstage edge to swing into the main room. Two steps, inside the door, lead up into the room. There is a pipe frame washstand downstage of the door against what would be the L. wall. It is used as a dressing table. A lamp with a small opaque shade, a small standing mirror, hairbrush, combs, etc., on this table. Two chamber vessels are visible; one under the cot, the other under the washstand. At the foot of the cot is a wooden box with a sewing basket on it, and a bulb with a frosted glass shade, hangs from the ceiling above. This light is controlled by a switch downstage on the door frame.

4

D. R. in the center room, with its back flush against the diagonal cut of the platform that is the Right room, is a small armless sofa. It is constructed so that a shelf may be pulled out from the base, forming a second sleeping space. Above the L. end of the sofa is a battered lamp table with a small lamp on it. The room is sparsely furnished; a rectangular table is c., there are two ladder backed chairs with wicker seats, two mismated chairs with wooden arms and upholstered seats, and a footstool with a padded top. Immediately above the door to the Right room, three steps rise to a small door. It swings offstage and leads to the W. C. When the W. C. light is on, it can be seen shining dimly through the window in the back wall of the Right room. The remainder of the u. R. wall consists of a fireplace with a rough wooden mantel. On the downstage end of the mantel is a small lamp. The opening of the fireplace has been plastered over but contains a sleeve to admit the pipe of a small, cylindrical, iron heating stove that stands in front of it. The top of this stove has a single, removable "lid" such as is found on old wood-burning cook-stoves. At the u. R. corner of the room, parallel to the footlights, is the kitchen area. A sink with a single, practical faucet is in the u. R. corner. The drainboard extends L. and a two burner gas hotplate has been placed on it. The wall above holds a shelf and hanging rack. There are pots, pans, skillets, and various utensils in evidence. Under the sink is a cabinet with two doors. It is used as a food chest. Upstage and behind the kitchen is a narrow curtained opening going off R. u. c., in the rear wall, is another large window. It has been boarded over. Only a small area in the upper L. corner remains clear. By standing on the first step of the stairs, which carry off u. L., a person can peer out. This flight of narrow steps leads to the Attic room. The upstage section of the L. wall is recessed and has four shelves built into it. Here is kept china, glassware, linen, medicine, brandy, an iron, etc. At the upstage end of these shelves are three hooks from which clothes may be hung. At L. c. is the door to the Left room. It is hinged upstage and opens into the Center room.

Downstage of this door is a short flight of stairs leading down to a door that is hinged upstage and swings on. When open, we can see the bookcase that camouflages the entrance from the office below. The handrail is upstage. This stairwell runs under the platform of the Left room. The Left room is supported in such a way that the audience can see down the stairwell to the door beneath. (NOTE: See first production note for possible elimination of stairs.) At c., hanging from the beam that is the supporting member under the attic room, hangs a bulb with a heavy metal shade slung under it. This shade is perforated to permit some direct light to shine through, but is primarily indirect in function. A wire is stretched, above head height, from the downstage edge of the L. shelf area, across the room to just below the sink. Two crude curtains of faded material hang from rings on this wire. If extended they would conceal the sink, staircase, shelf area from the remainder of the room. These curtains are usually pushed well open.

LEFT ROOM

Two steps, inside this room, lead up to a platform level. As you enter, a curtain upstage conceals a closet area. Downstage is another step that leads up to the bedroom level. Along what would be the R. wall, a bed has been constructed by putting a mattress on a door, supported by two boxes. A skylight, set at an angle, is D. L. and the wall upstage of it jogs diagonally onstage. This angular area contains another rise in the platform that gives the effect of an irregular window seat. At L. C. a fruit crate stands on end against the wall. It is used as a small table and storage space. A brass, goosenecked lamp is on the windowseat, and a blackout curtain of brown material is hanging below the skylight. The curtain can be lifted and hooked at the top edge of the sash to cover the dusty panes.

ATTIC ROOM

The stairwell opens into the extreme U. L. corner of the room. D. L. are several cardboard cartons, a small packing case, etc. C., in the rear, is a wardrobe built into the wall. A brass bed is D. R., headboard R., extending onstage. A person can move above the bed and get off R. out of the audience's view. A wall lamp with a glass shade, is R. of the wardrobe, and a small wooden stool is C. at the foot of the bed.

(NOTE: See Production Note for elimination of attic room, page 105.)

The Diary of Anne Frank

ACT I

SCENE 1

AT RISE: *The stage is dark. Slowly the lights fade up on the cyclorama revealing the rooftops of Amsterdam and the belfry tower. It is late afternoon November, 1945. Gradually the light in the rooms follows. The living area is in disarray, implying those who lived here made a hasty exit. In the Right room we can see the covering of the chaise is worn and faded. The cot* U. R. *has been stripped of covering, leaving the mattress exposed. The mirror is face down on the dressing table and no lamp is in evidence. The door is closed. In the Center room the sofa has a split in its back where springs and stuffing have broken through. There is no lamp on the lamp table. The padded footstool stands above the lamp table. A large map of the war area hangs over the fireplace.* U. R. *the curtain sags limply concealing most of the kitchen. A tattered curtain covers the* U. C. *window.* L., *the room dividing curtain is also extended. It has fallen to shreds with the passage of time, and partially conceals a straight back chair overturned behind it. One armchair is* L., *just above the stairwell. A ball of yarn and knitting needles have been left on it.* D. L. *the other armchair has been thrown over. At* C. *the table is overturned and* R. *of it the other straight chair lies on its side. An inexpertly knitted, multi-colored scarf hangs upstage of the* L. *door. A woman's white glove is on the floor by the lamp table. The Left room is bare, door ajar. A withered plant droops from a pot on the window seat. The cot is stripped, mat-*

7

tress exposed. The last fading rays of the sun come weakly through the skylight.

As the lights approach full we hear the melody of the carillon fading in and ship whistles in the distance. (Sound Cue 1.) After a moment the door at the foot of the stairwell swings open. Mr. Frank comes up the stairs. He is a gentle, cultured European in his middle years. There is a trace of a German accent in his speech. He is weak, ill, making a supreme effort at self-control. His clothes are threadbare. He carries a small rucksack. As he reaches the top of the stairs the chimes begin to strike six o'clock. (Sound Cue 2.) Mr. Frank moves slowly across to the couch where he puts down his rucksack. He moves U. R. and we can hear children outside begin a gay song as they play. (Sound Cue 2 continues.) He opens the door R. A street organ outside begins its jaunty air. (Sound Cue 2 concludes.) He closes the door and moves restlessly upstage, then L. The scarf catches his eye. He puts it around his neck. He wanders back toward the couch but stops as he sees the glove. He picks it up. Suddenly all control is gone. He breaks down, crying. Miep Gies comes up the stairs. She is a Dutch girl of about twenty-two, pregnant now. She gives one a feeling of great capacity and courage. She is compassionate and protective in her attitude toward Mr. Frank. She has been stenographer and secretary in his business. She has her coat and hat on, ready to go home. A small silver cross hangs at her throat.

MIEP. (*As she comes up the stairs.*) Are you all right, Mr. Frank?
MR. FRANK. (*Quickly controlling himself.*) Yes, Miep, yes.
MIEP. Everyone in the office has gone home. . . . It's after six. (*Moving C. above table, pleading.*) Don't stay up here, Mr. Frank. What's the use of torturing yourself like this?
MR. FRANK. I've come to say good-bye. . . . I'm leaving here, Miep.
MIEP. What do you mean? Where are you going? Where?
MR. FRANK. I don't know yet. I haven't decided.
MIEP. Mr. Frank, you can't leave here! This is your home! Amsterdam is your home. (*Mr. Frank crosses restlessly above to her*

L.) Your business is here, waiting for you. . . . You're needed here. . . . Now that the war is over, there are things that . . .

MR. FRANK. I can't stay in Amsterdam, Miep. It has too many memories for me. Everywhere there's something . . . the house we lived in . . . the school . . . the street organ playing out there . . . (*Moves wearily* D. L.) I'm not the person you used to know, Miep. I'm a bitter old man. (*Breaking off, he returns to her.*) Forgive me. I shouldn't speak to you like this . . . after all that you did for us . . . the suffering . . .

MIEP. No. No. It wasn't suffering. You can't say we suffered. (*As she speaks, she straightens a chair which is overturned.*)

MR. FRANK. I know what you went through, you and Mr. Kraler. I'll remember it as long as I live. (*He gives one last look around then starts for the steps.*) Come, Miep. (*Remembering his rucksack he crosses, below, to the couch. Light cue—trap out.*)

MIEP. (*Hurrying to the shelves* U. L.) Mr. Frank, did you see? There are some of your papers here. (*Crosses* D. L., *then* R. *to him, with a bundle of papers.*) We found them in a heap of rubbish on the floor after . . . after you left.

MR. FRANK. Burn them. (*He opens his rucksack to put the glove in it.*)

MIEP. But, Mr. Frank, there are letters, notes . . .

MR. FRANK. Burn them. All of them.

MIEP. Burn this? (*She hands him a worn, velour covered book.*)

MR. FRANK. (*Quietly.*) Anne's diary. (*He opens the diary and begins to read.*) "Monday, the sixth of July, nineteen hundred and forty-two." (*To Miep.*) Nineteen hundred and forty-two. Is it possible, Miep? . . . Only three years ago. "Dear Diary, since you and I are going to be great friends, I will start by telling you about myself. My name is Anne Frank. I am thirteen years old. (*He sits on couch.*) I was born in Germany the twelfth of June, nineteen-twenty-nine. As my family is Jewish, we emigrated to Holland when Hitler came to power." (*As Mr. Frank reads on, another Voice joins his, fading slowly in, as if coming from the air. It is Anne's voice, offstage on mike.*)

MR. FRANK AND ANNE. "My father started a business, importing spice and herbs. Things went well for us until 1940. Then the war came and the Dutch . . . (*He turns the page.*) defeat, followed by the arrival of the Germans. (*Lights start to fade, dim slow. Light cue.*) Then things got very bad for the Jews." (*All*

9

is dark now except one cool special vignetting Mr. Frank and Miep. His voice dies out as Anne continues stronger. Drop in, work light on, curtain light on, cellar light on.)

ANNE'S VOICE. You could not do this and you could not do that. *(Lag special dims out. Black scene drop is lowered.)* They forced Father out of his business. We had to wear yellow stars. I had to turn in my bike. I couldn't go to a Dutch school any more. I couldn't go to the movies, or ride in an automobile, or even on a streetcar, and a million other things. But somehow we children still managed to have fun. Yesterday Father told me we were going into hiding. Where he wouldn't say. At five o'clock this morning Mother woke me and told me to hurry and get dressed. I was to put on as many clothes as I could. It would look too suspicious if we walked along carrying suitcases. It wasn't until we were on our way that I learned where we were going. Our hiding place was to be upstairs . . . *(Work light off. Black drop rises.)* in the building where Father used to have his business. *(Drop out. Lights begin to fade up, cyclorama first, followed by playing area. Simultaneously Anne's voice begins slowly to fade out.)* Three other people were coming in with us . . . the Van Daans and their son Peter. . . . Father knew the Van Daans but we had never met them. . . . *(Dim up slow. Voice out, lights three-quarters full and rising. Ship whistles are heard. [Sound Cue 3.])*

ACT I

SCENE 2

Off L.: *Whistles at rise. (Sound Cue 4.)*

SCENE: *It is early morning, July, 1942. The photographs we saw at first, the war map, the dead plant, the knitting, are not there now. The rooms have been prepared for living. All beds are made, lamps in place, and furniture upright. The table* C. *is flanked by a straight chair* L., *an armchair* R. *The other straight chair is* U. R. *above the stove. The dividing curtains are partially drawn and, though far from new, are not in shreds.*

The three members of the Van Daan family are waiting for the Franks to arrive. Mr. Van Daan is a portly man

10

in his late forties. He is pacing u. c. in the center room smoking a cigarette, and watching his wife with a nervous eye. His overcoat and suit are expensive and well cut. Mrs. Van Daan sits on the couch, clutching her possessions, a hatbox, handbag, attractive straw carry-all. A cardboard carton is above her on the couch. It is tied with heavy cord. She is a pretty woman in her early forties. She wears a fur coat. Peter Van Daan is standing at the window of the Right room, looking down at the street below. He is a shy, awkward boy of sixteen. He wears a cap, a short overcoat, and long Dutch trousers, like "plus fours." At his feet is a black carrier with a cat in it. On the window seat is a small potted plant. His clothes have the conspicuous yellow Star of David on the left breast. The star is evident on his parents' clothing also. When lights are full, Mrs. Van Daan sneezes. Mr. Van Daan glances at her, then looks at his watch. He moves l., putting out his cigarette. She rises, crosses c., below the table, nervous, excited.

MRS. VAN DAAN. Something's happened to them. I know it. (*Warn cellar light off.*)

MR. VAN DAAN. (*Coming down to her.*) Now, Kerli!

MRS. VAN DAAN. Mr. Frank said they'd be here at seven o'clock. He said . . .

MR. VAN DAAN. They have two miles to walk. You can't expect . . . (*Cellar light off.*)

MRS. VAN DAAN. (*Overlapping.*) They've been picked up. . . . (*The door below opens.*) That's what's happened. They've been taken. (*Mr. Van Daan indicates that he hears someone coming.*)

MR. VAN DAAN. You see? (*Mr. Frank comes up the stairwell from below. He looks much younger now. His movements are brisk, his manner confident. He wears an overcoat and carries his hat and a small cardboard box.*)

MR. FRANK. Mrs. Van Daan, Mr. Van Daan. (*He crosses to the Van Daans, shaking hands with each of them. Peter has picked up his cat carrier and small plant, and comes into the center room. He stands outside the r. door. Mr. Frank continues up to Peter, shakes his hand. He puts carton on lamp table and comes back d. r. c. Mrs. Van Daan has crossed back to the sofa.*) There were

11

too many of the Green Police on the streets . . . we had to take the long way around. (*Miep, not pregnant now, Margot, Mr. Kraler, Mrs. Frank, have come up the stairs. Kraler carries two brief cases. He acknowledges the Van Daans and moves U. L. to the shelves, checking their contents. Miep and Margot cross to above the C. table. Miep empties her straw bag of the clothes it contains, piling them on R. end of table. Margot puts her leatherette carry-all and large brown paper bag on the table. Mrs. Frank also carries a leatherette shopping bag and her handbag. We see the Star of David conspicuous on the Franks' clothing. Margot is eighteen, beautiful, quiet, shy. Mrs. Frank is a young mother, gently bred, reserved. She, like Mr. Frank, has a slight German accent. Mr. Kraler is a Dutchman, dependable, kindly. He wears a hearing aid in his ear.*)

MRS. FRANK. (*Calling down the stairs.*) Anne? (*Anne comes quickly up the stairs. She is thirteen, quick in her movements, interested in everything, mercurial in her emotions. She wears a cape, long wool socks and carries a school bag.*)

MR. FRANK. (*Crossing to C. below table.*) My wife, Edith. Mr. and Mrs. Van Daan. (*Mrs. Frank shakes Mr. Van Daan's hand, then hurries across to shake hands with Mrs. Van Daan. She then crosses up to inspect the sink.*) . . . their son, Peter . . . my daughters, Margot, and Anne. (*Anne gives a polite little curtsey as she shakes Mr. Van Daan's hand. She puts her bag on L. end of C. table. Then she immediately starts off on a tour of investigation of her new home, going upstairs to the attic room. Mr. Van Daan sits L. of table, fanning himself. Miep crosses to sink, places thermos of milk on drain board.*)

KRALER. (*Crossing R. above table and downstage to Mr. Frank.*) I'm sorry there is still so much confusion.

MR. FRANK. Please. Don't think of it. After all, we'll have plenty of leisure to arrange everything ourselves. (*Kraler crosses up to Right room, enters and places briefcases on floor by dressing table.*)

MIEP. (*Indicates sink cupboard first, then moves L. toward shelves. Mr. Frank crosses up to mantel, puts hat on it. He moves across to shelves after Miep. Mrs. Frank also comes to the shelves. Margot takes bag of food to sink chest and puts items in it.*) We put the stores of food you sent in here. Your drugs are here . . . soap, linen, here.

MRS. FRANK. Thank you, Miep.

MIEP. I made up the beds . . . the way Mr. Frank and Mr. Kraler said. (*Hurries toward stairwell. Mr. Kraler, having inspected the Right room, re-enters the Center room and crosses down to the sofa.*) Forgive me. I have to hurry. I've got to go to the othe: side of town to get some ration books for you.

MRS. VAN DAAN. (*Rises.*) Ration books? If they see our names on ration books, they'll know we're here. (*Mr. Kraler and Miep speak together.*)

KRALER. There isn't anything . . .

MIEP. Don't worry. Your names won't be on them. (*As she hurries out.*) I'll be up later.

MR. FRANK. (*Crosses to stairwell watching her leave.*) Thank you, Miep.

MRS. FRANK. (*Troubled, crossing down L. then to C. To Kraler.*) It's illegal, then, the ration books? We've never done anything illegal.

MR. FRANK. We won't be living exactly according to regulations here. (*Kraler moves C. to Mrs. Frank. As he speaks reassuringly to her, he takes several small bottles of medicine from his coat pockets and gives them to her.*)

MR. KRALER. This isn't the black market, Mrs. Frank. This is what we call the white market . . . helping all of the hundreds and hundreds who are hiding out in Amsterdam. (*The carillon is heard playing the quarter hour before eight. [Sound Cue 5.] Mr. Kraler looks at his watch. Anne stops at the window as she comes down the stairs, and looks out through the curtains.*)

ANNE. It's the Westertoren!

MR. KRALER. I must go. (*Goes up to Peter, shakes his hand, then down again to shake Mrs. Van Daan's. Anne is inspecting the kitchen area. Margot returns to above C. table.*) I must be out of here and downstairs in the office before the workmen get here. Miep or I, or both of us, will be up each day to bring you food and news and find out what your needs are. (*Crossing L., Mr. Frank waits for him just downstage of the stairwell.*) Tomorrow I'll get you a better bolt for the door at the foot of the stairs. It needs a bolt that you can throw yourself and open only at our signal. (*To Mr. Frank.*) Oh. . . . You'll tell them about the noise?

13

MR. FRANK. I'll tell them.

MR. KRALER. Good-bye then for the moment. I'll come up again, after the workmen leave.

MR. FRANK. (Shaking Kraler's hand.) Good-bye, Mr. Kraler.

MRS. FRANK. (Shaking his hand.) How can we thank you?

MR. KRALER. I never thought I'd live to see the day when a man like Mr. Frank would have to go into hiding. When you think ——— (He breaks off and goes out. Mr. Frank follows him down the steps, bolting the door after him. In the interval before he returns, Peter goes over to Margot, gives a stiff bow as they shake hands. Anne has been U. C. watching and as they complete their greeting she moves down to Peter, hand extended. He has turned away and does not see her. Mrs. Frank drifts thoughtfully U. L. As Mr. Frank comes back up the stairs she hurries down to him.)

MRS. FRANK. What did he mean, about the noise?

MR. FRANK. First let's take off some of these clothes. (He crosses to the chair above the iron stove, placing his overcoat on it. Anne goes down R. of the table, ending C. below with her back to the audience. She places her cape and beret on the pile of clothes. They all start to take off garment after garment. On each of their coats, sweaters, blouses, suits, dresses, is another yellow Star of David. Mr. and Mrs. Frank are under-dressed quite simply. The others wear several things, sweaters, extra dresses, bathrobes, aprons, etc. Mrs. Frank takes off her gloves, carefully folding them before putting them away.)

MR. VAN DAAN. (Crossing to sofa.) It's a wonder we weren't arrested, walking along the streets. . . . Petronella with a fur coat in July . . . and that cat of Peter's crying all the way.

ANNE. (As she is removing a pair of panties.) A cat?

MRS. FRANK. (Shocked.) Anne, please!

ANNE. It's all right. I've got on three more. (She removes two more pairs of panties. Mr. Frank crosses L. above, then to D. L. Finally, as they finish removing their surplus clothes, they settle down. Mrs. Frank sits L. of table, Anne sits on the table, C., feet dangling. Margot stands above. Mr. and Mrs. Van Daan sit on sofa, Peter is by R. door where he has placed his clothes on the stool.)

MR. FRANK. Now. About the noise. While the men are in the building below, we must have complete quiet. Every sound can be heard down there, not only in the workrooms, but in the offices

14

too. The men come about eight-thirty, and leave at about five-thirty. So, to be perfectly safe, from eight in the morning until six in the evening we must move only when it is necessary and then in stockinged feet. (*Crossing to R. C. below table.*) We must not speak above a whisper. We must not run any water. We cannot use the sink, or even, forgive me, the W. C. The pipes go down through the workrooms. It would be heard. No trash . . . (*The sound of marching feet stops Mr. Frank. [Sound Cue 6.] He goes into the bedroom stage R., followed by Anne, and peers out of the window. Satisfied that the marching feet are going away, he returns and continues. Anne follows him and curls up in chair R. of table.*) No trash must ever be thrown out which might reveal that someone is living here . . . not even a potato paring. We must burn everything in the stove at night. This is the way we must live until it is over, if we are to survive. (*He moves R. There is a pause. Margot accidentally drops the nightgown she is taking off. Peter jumps to pick it up for her. He then crosses to above L. end of table.*)

MRS. FRANK. Until it is over.

MR. FRANK. After six we can move about . . . we can talk and laugh and have our supper and read and play games . . . just as we would at home. (*He looks at his watch.*) And now I think it would be wise if we all went to our rooms, and were settled before eight o'clock. Mrs. Van Daan, you and your husband will be upstairs. I regret that there's no place up there for Peter. But he will be here, near us. This will be our common room, where we'll meet to talk and eat and read, like one family.

MRS. VAN DAAN. And where do you and Mrs. Frank sleep?

MR. FRANK. This room is also our bedroom.

(*Together.*)

| MRS. VAN DAAN. (*She rises in protest and crosses to Mr. Frank carrying coat, hatbox, and straw bag.*) That isn't right. We'll sleep here and you take the room upstairs. | MR. VAN DAAN. It's your place. |

MR. FRANK. Please. I've thought this out for weeks. It's the best arrangement. The only arrangement. (*Mr. Van Daan starts to load his arms with the clothes he and his wife have taken off and thrown across the sofa.*)

15

MRS. VAN DAAN. (*To Mr. Frank, as she shakes his hand.*) Never, never can we thank you. (*Then to Mrs. Frank, shaking her hand.*) I don't know what would have happened to us, if it hadn't been for Mr. Frank.

MR. FRANK. You don't know how your husband helped me when I came to this country . . . knowing no one . . . not able to speak the language. I can never repay him for that. (*Going to Van Daan.*) May I help you with your things?

MR. VAN DAAN. No. No. (*To Mrs. Van Daan, as he picks up carton and starts U. C. toward stairs.*) Come along, Liefje.

MRS. VAN DAAN. You'll be all right, Peter? You're not afraid?

PETER. (*Embarrassed, he moves R., picks up his gear. Mrs. Frank steps to head of stairwell and stares thoughtfully down.*) Please, Mother. (*Mr. and Mrs. Van Daan go upstairs. Mr. Frank moves to C. above table.*)

MR. FRANK. You too must have some rest, Edith. You didn't close your eyes last night. Nor you, Margot.

ANNE. I slept, Father. Wasn't that funny? I knew it was the last night in my own bed, and yet I slept soundly. (*Peter carries his gear over L., placing it on chair downstage of L. door. Cat case is set on floor.*)

MR. FRANK. I'm glad, Anne. Now you'll be able to help me straighten things in here. (*To Mrs. Frank and Margot.*) Come with me. . . . You and Margot rest in this room for the time being. (*Opens door of Right room.*)

MRS. FRANK. (*Crossing R., above, toward him.*) You're sure . . . ? I could help, really. . . . And Anne hasn't had her milk. . . .

MR. FRANK. I'll give it to her. (*To Anne and Peter, as he comes to table, picks up the pile of clothes left by Miep, Anne and Margot.*) Anne, Peter . . . it's best that you take off your shoes now, before you forget. (*He leads the way to the Right room with Margot. He turns on light, wall switch. She brings her bag. Light cue. Anne's bracket—Frank.*)

MRS. FRANK. You're sure you're not tired, Anne?

ANNE. (*She and Peter are taking off shoes.*) I feel fine. I'm going to help Father.

MRS. FRANK. Peter, I'm glad you are to be with us.

PETER. Yes, Mrs. Frank. (*Mrs. Frank follows Mr. Frank and Margot into room R.; closes door. During the following scene Mr.*

16

Frank helps Margot hang up the clothes he has piled on cot U. R. Coats, hats in window seat. Skirts, sweaters, blouses on pegs above window. Takes pillow from chest for Margot's bed, puts remainder of clothes into drawer. Moves Kraler's bags and Margot's bag below dressing table. Margot puts comb, brush, etc., on dressing table, then lies down on rear wall cot. Mrs. Frank carefully folds her things on box at foot of bed D. C., then lies down. All this is unhurried. Peter takes his cat out of its case.)

ANNE. *(She crosses to him.)* What's your cat's name?

PETER. *(Self-conscious, shy.)* Mouschi.

ANNE. *(to the cat.)* Mouschi! Mouschi! Mouschi! *(She picks up the cat, walks away above the table, swings down R., then to C. below table.)* I love cats. I have one . . . a darling little cat. But they made me leave her behind. I left some food and a note for the neighbors to take care of her. . . . I'm going to miss her terribly. What is yours? A him or a her?

PETER. *(Crossing down, then to C.)* He's a tom. He doesn't like strangers. *(He takes the cat from her, putting it back in its carrier.)*

ANNE. *(Unabashed, she follows after him.)* Then I'll have to stop being a stranger, won't I? Is he fixed?

PETER. *(Startled.)* Huh?

ANNE. Did you have him fixed?

PETER. No.

ANNE. Oh, you ought to have him fixed—to keep him from fighting. Where did you go to school?

PETER. Jewish Secondary.

ANNE. But that's where Margot and I go! I never saw you around.

PETER. I used to see you . . . sometimes. . . .

ANNE. You did?

PETER. . . . in the school yard. You were always in the middle of a bunch of kids. *(He takes a penknife from his pocket.)*

ANNE. Why didn't you ever come over?

PETER. I'm sort of a lone wolf. *(He starts to rip off his Star of David.)*

ANNE. What are you doing?

PETER. Taking it off.

ANNE. But you can't do that. *(Grabs his hands, stopping him.)* They'll arrest you if you go out without your star.

PETER. Who's going out? *(He pulls away and brushes by her to*

17

C. *He puts his knife on table, then goes up to stove. He lifts lid, throws star into stove.*)

ANNE. Why, of course! You're right! Of course we don't need them any more. (*Crossing to above table, she picks up his knife and starts to take off her star. He waits for hers, to throw it away.*) I wonder what our friends will think when we don't show up today?

PETER. I didn't have any dates with anyone.

ANNE. (*Facing front above table, concentrating on her star.*) Oh, I did. I had a date with Jopie this afternoon to go and play pingpong at her house. Do you know Jopie deWaal?

PETER. No. (*Warn L6. Anne's bracket—Frank.*)

ANNE. Jopie's my best friend. I wonder what she'll think when she telephones and there's no answer? . . . Probably she'll go over to the house. . . . I wonder what she'll think . . . we left everything as if we'd suddenly been called away . . . breakfast dishes in the sink . . . beds not made . . . (*As she pulls off her star, the cloth underneath shows clearly the color and form of the star.*) Look! (*Puts knife on table.*) It's still there! (*Peter comes to her R. to have a look. Picks up knife and puts it in his pocket.*) What're you going to do with yours?

PETER. Burn it. (*Moving back to stove, he holds out his hand for her star.*)

ANNE. (*She starts to give it to him, but cannot. Steps back to C. above table.*) It's funny, I can't throw it away. I don't know why.

PETER. (*A step down, incredulous.*) You can't throw . . . ? Something they branded you with . . . ? That they made you wear so they could spit on you?

ANNE. I know. I know. But after all, it is the Star of David, isn't it? (*Light cue. Anne's bracket—Frank. The Van Daans have arranged their things, clothes in wardrobe, and are sitting on the bed fanning themselves. The chores are completed in the Right room. Mr. Frank turns out the light and goes into the Center room. He closes the door quietly.*)

PETER. Maybe it's different for a girl.

MR. FRANK. (*Crosses C., Anne puts her star in her school bag.*) Forgive me, Peter. Now let me see. We must find a bed for your cat. (*Peter comes down to above table. Anne kneels, looking into Mouschi's case.*) I'm glad you brought your cat. Anne was feel-

18

ing so badly about hers. (*He sees a small worn wash tub and pulls it from the top shelf* U. L., *then returns, giving it to Peter. Anne wanders* R. *below table, inspecting everything. She kneels on upstage end of sofa, giving it a thorough examination.*) Here we are. Will it be comfortable in that?

PETER. Thanks.

MR. FRANK. (*Indicating the Left room.*) And here is your room. But I warn you, Peter, you can't grow any more. Not an inch, or you'll have to sleep with your feet out of the skylight. (*Mr. Frank goes to the door and opens it. Peter follows and puts the tub inside.*) Are you hungry?

PETER. (*Gathering up his things from chair and floor.*) No.

MR. FRANK. We have some bread and butter?

PETER. No, thank you.

MR. FRANK. (*A friendly pat on Peter's shoulder.*) You can have it for luncheon then. And tonight we will have a real supper . . . our first supper together.

PETER. Thanks. Thanks. (*He goes off into his room. Mr. Frank closes the door after him.*)

MR. FRANK. (*Sitting* L. *of table, removing his shoes.*) That's a nice boy, Peter.

ANNE. He's awfully shy, isn't he?

MR. FRANK. You'll like him, I know.

ANNE. (*Crossing above table to him.*) I certainly hope so, since he's the only boy I'm likely to see for months and months.

MR. FRANK. Anne, there's a box there. Will you open it? (*Anne goes over to the carton on the lamp table, and brings it back to the* C. *table. In the street we begin to hear children playing.* [*Sound Cue 7.*] *Mr. Frank goes to the sink, pouring a glass of milk from the thermos bottle.*)

ANNE. (*Sound of children playing offstage.*) You know the way I'm going to think of it here? I'm going to think of it as a boarding house. A very peculiar summer boarding house, like the one that we —— (*She breaks off as she looks in the box.*) Father! Father! My movie stars! I was wondering where they were! . . . and Queen Wilhelmina! How wonderful! (*Mr. Frank returns to her* L., *placing glass on* D. L. *corner of table.*)

MR. FRANK. There's something more. Go on. Look further.

ANNE. (*She digs deeper into the box and brings out a velour covered book. She examines it in delighted silence for a moment,*

19

then opens the cover slowly. She looks up at him with eyes shining.) A diary! *(She throws her arms around him.)* I've never had a diary. And I've always longed for one. *(She rushes to the lamp table R., looking for a pencil.)* Pencil, pencil, pencil, pencil. *(Darting across the room, below C. table, she starts for the stairs.)* I'm going down to the office to get a pencil. *(Curtain light on.)*

MR. FRANK. Anne! No! *(Mr. Frank has started back to replace the cap on the thermos. He turns and strides L. and down, catching her arm as she starts down the stairs. He pulls her back and toward C. Mrs. Frank, in the Right bedroom, sits up, aware of the sudden movement and sound. After a moment she goes to the window and looks out. She returns and sits on the bed.)*

ANNE. *(Startled.)* But there's no one in the building now.

MR. FRANK. It doesn't matter. I don't want you ever to go beyond that door.

ANNE. *(Sobered.)* Never? . . . Not even at night time, when everyone is gone? Or on Sundays? Can't I go down to listen to the radio?

MR. FRANK. Never. I am sorry, Anneke. It isn't safe. No, you must never go beyond that door. *(For the first time Anne realizes what "going into hiding" means.)*

ANNE. I see.

MR. FRANK. It'll be hard, I know. But always remember this, Anneke. There are no walls, there are no bolts, no locks that anyone can put on your mind. Miep will bring us books. We will read history, poetry, mythology. *(He gives her the glass of milk.)* Here's your milk. *(With his arm about her, they go over to the couch, sitting down side by side.)* As a matter of fact, between us, Anne, being here has certain advantages for you. For instance, you remember the battle you had with your mother the other day on the subject of overshoes? You said you'd rather die than wear overshoes. But in the end you had to wear them? Well now, you see for as long as we are here you will never have to wear overshoes! Isn't that good? And the coat that you inherited from Margot . . . *(She makes a wry face.)* you won't have to wear that. And the piano! You won't have to practice on the piano. I tell you, this is going to be a fine life for you! *(Anne's panic is gone. Peter appears in the doorway of his room, with a saucer in his hand. He is carrying his cat.)*

20

PETER. I . . . I . . . I thought I'd better get some water for Mouschi before . . . (*Mr. Frank rises from sofa.*)

MR. FRANK. (*Starting for the sink.*) Of course. (*As he moves toward the sink the carillon begins its melody before striking eight. [Sound Cue 8.] He motions for the children to be quiet, tiptoes to the window in the rear wall, and peers down. Mr. Van Daan, in the Attic room, has crossed to the head of the stairs. Mr. Frank puts his finger to his lips, indicating to Anne and Peter that they must be silent, then steps down toward Peter indicating he can draw no water. Peter starts back to his room. Anne starts to move R. below table with her milk and the diary. Mr. Frank crosses quietly toward the R. room. As Peter reaches the door of his room a board creaks under his foot. The three are frozen for a minute in fear. Anne then continues over to Peter on tiptoe and pours some milk in the saucer. Peter squats on the floor, putting the milk before the cat, encouraging him to drink. Mr. Frank comes back to them, giving Anne his fountain pen. He then crosses back to the Right room and sits on the bed downstage, a comforting arm around Mrs. Frank. For a second time Anne squats beside Peter, watching the cat, then she goes to the chair R. of the table, puts down the glass, climbs into the chair with her feet tucked under her, and, opening her diary, begins to write. All the people are silent, motionless except Mr. Van Daan who has returned to his wife and is fanning her with a newspaper. The Westertoren finishes tolling the hour. As Anne begins to write the scene lights fade and we hear her voice, [Lights dim slowly. Drop in.] faintly at first, and then with growing strength. Work light on. Curtain light on.*)*

ANNE'S VOICE. I expect I should be describing what it feels like to go into hiding. (*Scene lights out, leaving Anne in a small pool of light from a lag special.*) But I really don't know yet myself. (*Lag special fades out. Black scene curtain is brought in. Voice is full.*) I only know it's funny never to be able to go outdoors . . . never to breathe fresh air . . . never to run and shout and jump. It's the silence in the night that frightens me most. Every time I hear a creak in the house, or a step on the street outside, I'm sure they're coming for us. The days aren't so bad. At least we know that Miep and Mr. Kraler are down there below us in the office. Our protectors we call them. I asked Father what would happen to them if the Nazis found out they were hiding us. (*W. L. off.*) Pim said that they would suffer the same fate that

we would. . . . Imagine! They know this and yet when they come
up here, they're always cheerful and gay as if there were nothing
in the world to bother them. . . . (*Drop up.*) Friday, the twenty-
first of August, nineteen-forty-two. (*Black drop is taken out and
lights begin a slow fade up. Voice begins a slow fade out.*) Today
I'm going to tell you our general news. (*Dim slow.*) Mother is
unbearable! She insists on treating me like a baby, which I loathe.
(*Voice fades out. Lights are three-quarters full and rising. Warn
£81 W. C.*) Otherwise things are going better. The weather is . . .

ACT I

SCENE 3

Off stage L.: *WHISTLES ON RISE. TOOTS.* (*Sound
Cue 9.*)
SCENE: *It is a few minutes after six o'clock in the evening,
two months later. The furniture arrangement is as in pre-
ceding scene except that a straight chair has been moved
to above the* C. *table. A stack of books has appeared on
Peter's window seat. The dividing curtains are wide open
and Anne's and Peter's shoes are on the floor in front of
the* C. *table. The table lamp in Anne's room is on. Mrs.
Frank's knitting is on the lamp table. A bowl of green
beans, yet to be snapped, is on the drainboard. A pot is
on the hotplate.*
*In the Center room Mr. Frank, with his shoes in his hand,
stands at the window looking down at the street below,
waiting to see that the workmen have left the building.
The group in the room watch him intently, waiting for
his signal to be able to move. Mrs. Van Daan sits in the
chair above the stairwell, her fur coat in her lap. Anne
and Peter are seated opposite each other at the center
table, where they have been doing lessons in copybooks.
He is* R., *she is* L. *Mrs. Frank stands above the couch,
shoes in hand, waiting to put them on. From outside we
hear the sounds of street traffic and canal sounds. (Sound
Cue 10.) Margot is seated at the dressing table in the*

22

Right bedroom, where she is studying. Mr. Van Daan is in the Attic room above playing solitaire on the bed. After a couple of seconds of silence, Mr. Frank turns from the window.

MR. FRANK. (*Quietly, to the group.*) It's safe now. The last workman has left. (*There is an immediate stir of relief and activity among the people in the main room.*)

ANNE. (*Throwing her arms and legs wide in an exaggerated gesture of relief.*) Whee!

MRS. FRANK. (*Startled, amused.*) Anne!

MRS. VAN DAAN. I'm first for the W. C. (*She hurries across to the W. C., pausing only long enough to drape her coat carefully over the chair above the C. table. Inside the W. C. she turns on the light. Mrs. Frank puts on her shoes and starts up to the sink to prepare supper. She puts on her apron and begins beating a bowl of batter. Anne sneaks Peter's shoes from under the table as he stretches, and hides them behind her back. Mr. Frank, carrying his shoes, goes in to Margot's room.*)

MR. FRANK. (*To Margot.*) Six o'clock. School's over. (*Margot gets up, stretching. Mr. Frank sits on the downstage bed to put on his shoes. In the Center room Anne is watching as Peter tries to find his shoes. He remains seated as he peers under the table.*)

PETER. (*To Anne.*) Have you seen my shoes?

ANNE. (*Innocently.*) Your shoes?

PETER. (*He knows.*) You've taken them, haven't you?

ANNE. I don't know what you're talking about.

PETER. (*Half rising as he prepares to catch her.*) You're going to be sorry!

ANNE. Am I? (*She holds the shoes tightly and makes a feint as if to run upstage. Peter lunges above the table to catch her. Anne reverses and runs below the table and to her mother U. C. who is watching with amusement. Peter continues his circle of the table hot on her heels, but is slowed as he becomes entangled in the R. chair Anne pulls into his path. She is hiding behind Mrs. Frank but Peter manages to catch her hands. They fall to the floor U. L. Warn L 82. Anne lamp off.*)

MRS. FRANK. (*Protesting.*) Anne, dear!

PETER. Wait till I get you!

ANNE. I'm waiting! (*Peter pins her down, wrestling to get the*

23

shoes. All through this action Anne has been having a wonderful time.) Don't! Don't! Peter, stop it. Ouch!

MRS. FRANK. Anne! . . . Peter! (*Suddenly Peter becomes self-conscious. He grabs his shoes roughly and starts for his room.*)

ANNE. (*Catching him as he opens the door.*) Peter, where are you going? Come dance with me.

PETER. I tell you I don't know how.

ANNE. I'll teach you.

PETER. I'm going to give Mouschi his dinner.

ANNE. Can I watch?

PETER. He doesn't like people around while he eats.

ANNE. Peter, please.

PETER. No! (*He goes into his room. Anne slams his door after him.*)

MRS. FRANK. Anne dear, I think you shouldn't play like that with Peter. It's not dignified.

ANNE. (*She is deflated now and crosses above C. table inspecting her chafed elbows. Site L 82. Anne lamp off—Frank.*) Who cares if it's dignified? I don't want to be dignified. (*Anne throws herself across the chair R. of the table in a most undignified manner. In the Right room Mr. Frank turns off the lamp on the dressing table and Margot gives him her copybook. They enter the Center room. Margot goes up to help Mrs. Frank. He crosses below the C. table gathering up Anne's copybooks. Peter is putting on his shoes in his own room.*)

MRS. FRANK. (*To Anne.*) You complain that I don't treat you like a grownup. But when I do, you resent it. (*Mrs. Frank sits L. of the table. Margot brings a cloth down and wipes table. Anne replaces R. chair at the table.*)

ANNE. I only want some fun . . . someone to laugh and clown with. . . . After you've sat still all day and hardly moved, you've got to have some fun. I don't know what's the matter with that boy.

MR. FRANK. He isn't used to girls. Give him a little time.

ANNE. (*Warn L 83. W. C. off.*) Time? Isn't two months time? I could cry. (*Catching hold of Margot as she starts back to the sink.*) Come on, Margot . . . dance with me. Come on, please.

MARGOT. (*Pulling away, she returns to her duties with Mrs. Frank.*) I have to help with supper.

ANNE. You know we're going to forget how to dance. . . . When we get out we won't remember a thing. (*She sings to herself, "Ta-*

24

dum, Ja-dum, Ja-dum, Dum-dum." She waltzes down to below
the L. end of the table then to C. Mr. Frank has crossed to C. below
the table looking at Peter's copybook. As Anne approaches he
holds out his arms and they do a few turns of a waltz D. C. Mrs.
Van Daan turns off the W. C. light and comes to above the table.)

MRS. VAN DAAN. (As she enters.) Next? (She looks around
as she starts putting on her shoes.) Where's Peter?

ANNE. Where would he be! (Mr. Frank and Anne finish with a
flourish and a bow. Anne continues singing quietly, circles L. and
up to U. L. C. Mr. Frank resumes his seat L. and begins to check
the lessons.)

MRS. VAN DAAN. He hasn't finished his lessons, has he? His
father'll kill him if he catches him in there with that cat and his
work not done. (Picking up her fur coat and going to the sofa
where she sits.) Anne, get him out of there, will you?

ANNE. (Dances quickly to Peter's door and knocks in rhythm to
her singing. "Ja-dum, Ja-dum, Ja-dum, Knock-knock.") Peter?
Peter?

PETER. (Opening the door a crack.) What is it?

ANNE. Your mother says to come out.

PETER. I'm giving Mouschi his dinner.

MRS. VAN DAAN. You know what your father says. (She ar-
ranges the coat carefully over her lap, caressing the fur, touching
her cheek with the collar.)

PETER. For heaven's sake, I haven't even looked at him since
lunch.

MRS. VAN DAAN. I'm just telling you, that's all.

ANNE. I'll feed him.

PETER. I don't want you in there.

MRS. VAN DAAN. Peter!

PETER. (To Anne.) Then give him his dinner and come right out,
you hear? (He comes back to his chair R. of the table, crossing
above. Anne shuts the door of Peter's room after her and disap-
pears behind the curtain covering his closet.)

MRS. VAN DAAN. (To Peter.) Now is that any way to talk to
your little girl friend?

PETER. (He sits.) Mother . . . for heaven's sake . . . will you
please stop saying that?

MRS. VAN DAAN. Look at him blush! Look at him!

25

PETER. (*Uncomfortable.*) Please! I'm not . . . anyway . . . let me alone, will you?

MRS. VAN DAAN. He acts like it was something to be ashamed of. It's nothing to be ashamed of, to have a little girl friend.

PETER. You're crazy. She's only thirteen.

MRS. VAN DAAN. So what? And you're sixteen. Just perfect. Your father's ten years older than I am. (*To Mr. Frank.*) I warn you, Mr. Frank, if this war lasts much longer, you and I are going to be related.

MR. FRANK. Mazeltov!

MRS. FRANK. (*Deliberately, as she comes down to R. of the table.*) I wonder where Miep is? She's usually so prompt. (*Suddenly everything else is forgotten as they listen to a sound in the street. It is the sound of an automobile coming to a sudden stop. [Sound Cue 11.] The people in the room are tense, motionless in their terror. The car starts away. A wave of relief sweeps over the people. Mrs. Frank returns to her dinner preparations. Mr. Frank goes back to the copybooks. Suddenly Anne flings open the door of Peter's room, making a dramatic entrance. She is dressed in Peter's "plus-fours," jacket and cap. She affects a long stride and a deep voice as she crosses below the table then circles to the chair above. Peter looks at her in fury. The others are amused.*)

ANNE. Good evening, everyone. Forgive me if I don't stay. I have a friend waiting for me in there. My friend Tom, Tom Cat. (*She hops up on the chair putting one foot on the table.*) Some people say that we look alike. But Tom has the most beautiful whiskers . . . (*She strokes her imaginary whiskers. Peter starts to cross above her to his room.*) and I have only a little fuzz. I am hoping . . . in time . . .

PETER. (*Wheeling on her, he comes to her L.*) All right, Mrs. Quack Quack!

ANNE. (*Outraged—jumping down and pushing him away.*) Peter!

PETER. I heard about you. . . . How you talked so much in class they called you Mrs. Quack Quack. (*Crossing R. below, to get the copybook he has left on the table.*) How Mr. Smitter made you write a composition . . . "'Quack, quack,' said Mrs. Quack Quack."

ANNE. Well, go on. Tell them the rest. (*She pursues him and gives him another shove as he gets the book. She uses both hands and the trousers fall to her ankles. She hitches them up and continues after him as he crosses above to the door of his room.*) How it was so good he read it out loud to the class and then read it to all his other classes!

PETER. Quack! Quack! Quack . . . Quack . . . Quack . . . (*Anne pulls off the coat and trousers.*)

ANNE. You are the most intolerable, insufferable boy I've ever met! (*She throws the clothes down the stairwell. Peter quickly places his book just inside the door of his room and goes after them.*)

MRS. VAN DAAN. (*To Anne . . . as she rises and moves up to help with the supper preparations. Her coat is left on the sofa.*) That's right, Anneke! Give it to him!

ANNE. (*She slumps in the chair above the stairwell.*) With all the boys in the world . . . . Why I had to get locked up with one like you!

PETER. Quack, quack, quack, and from now on stay out of my room! (*As Peter speaks he comes up the stairs and starts to his room. Anne puts out her foot, tripping him. He picks himself up, furious and inarticulate, and takes the clothes into his closet. The door is left open. Anne is all innocence. Mrs. Frank comes down to smooth Anne's hair. In doing so she feels Anne's forehead.*)

MRS. FRANK. (*Quietly.*) Anne, dear . . . your hair. You're warm. Are you feeling all right?

ANNE. (*Pulling away she goes to her shoes and slips into them.*) Please, Mother.

MRS. FRANK. You haven't a fever, have you?

ANNE. (*Mrs. Frank crosses toward her above the table. Anne moves R. to the sofa.*) No. No.

MRS. FRANK. Anneke, dear, don't do that. You know we can't call a doctor here, ever. There's only one thing to do . . . watch carefully. Prevent an illness before it comes. (*Anne turns her back on her mother as Mrs. Frank comes to her L.*) Let me see your tongue.

ANNE. Mother, this is perfectly absurd.

MRS. FRANK. Anne dear, don't be such a baby. Let me see your tongue. (*As Anne refuses, Mrs. Frank appeals to Mr. Frank.*) Otto . . . ?

MR. FRANK. You hear your mother, Anne. (*Anne turns her head*

27

toward her mother, sticks out her tongue for an instant, and immediately turns away.)

MRS. FRANK. (*Good-naturedly.*) Come on—open up! (*Since she must, Anne goes all the way . . . tongue out as far as possible, mouth wide, leaning toward her mother.*) You seem all right . . . but perhaps an aspirin . . . (*Mrs. Frank goes back to the sink. Anne follows her. Mrs. Van Daan moves to above* C. *table. Mr. Van Daan, having put his cards away, comes downstairs.*)

MRS. VAN DAAN. For Heaven's sake don't give that child any pills. I waited for fifteen minutes this morning for her to come out of the W. C.

ANNE. I was washing my hair!

MR. FRANK. (*As Mrs. Van Daan returns to couch and sits.*) I think there's nothing the matter with our Anne that a ride on her bike, or a visit with Jopie de Waal wouldn't cure. Isn't that so, Anne? (*Anne gives her father a hug. Mr. Van Daan moves down toward Mrs. Van Daan. We hear a fleet of bombers high overhead.*) [Sound Cue 12.]

MR. VAN DAAN. Miep not come yet?

MRS. VAN DAAN. The workmen just left, a little while ago.

MR. VAN DAAN. (*As he makes a* L. *turn below the* C. *table.*) What's for dinner tonight?

MRS. VAN DAAN. Beans.

MR. VAN DAAN. (*Stops short, throws a pained look back at his wife.*) Not again!

MRS. VAN DAAN. Poor Putti! I know. But what can we do? That's all that Miep brought us. (*Mr. Van Daan resumes his pacing, moving* L. *Anne has come quickly down behind him and follows him, imitating his posture and stride as he starts moving up toward Peter's open door.*)

ANNE. (*Again the deep voice.*) We are now in what is known as the "bean cycle." Beans boiled, beans en casserole, beans with strings, beans without strings . . . (*Mr. Van Daan sticks his head into Peter's room just as Peter starts out.*)

MR. VAN DAAN. (*To Peter.*) I saw you . . . in there, playing with your cat. (*Peter crosses above the* C. *table, sits in his chair* R. *of it.*)

MRS. VAN DAAN. (*Again she has the coat spread across her lap and is stroking the fur.*) He just went in for a second, putting his coat away. He's been out here all the time, doing his lessons.

MR. FRANK. (*Looking up from the papers.*) Anne, you got an excellent in your history paper today . . . and very good in Latin. (*Mr. Van Daan paces* R. *in a pattern that will circle* D. R., *across below the table then* U. L. *again. His pacing reminds us of a caged animal.*)

ANNE. (*Sitting beside Mr. Frank, above the table.*) How about algebra?

MR. FRANK. I'll have to make a confession. Up until now I've managed to stay ahead of you in algebra. Today you caught up with me. We'll leave it to Margot to correct.

ANNE. Isn't algebra *vile*, Pim!

MR. FRANK. Vile!

MARGOT. (*To Mr. Frank, as she moves between them.*) How did I do?

ANNE. (*Getting up and patting Margot on the head.*) Excellent, excellent, excellent, excellent! (*Margot brushes away Anne's hand. Anne moves away,* R.)

MR. FRANK. (*To Margot.*) You should have used the subjunctive here. . . .

MARGOT. Should I? . . . I thought . . . look here . . . I didn't use it here. . . . (*The two become absorbed in the papers Margot sits in chair vacated by Anne.*)

ANNE. (*Coming down to the sofa.*) Mrs. Van Daan, may I try on your coat?

MRS. FRANK. (*A step toward Anne.*) No, Anne.

MRS. VAN DAAN. (*Holding it up so Anne can slip into it.*) It's all right . . . but careful with it. My father gave me that the year before he died. He always bought the best that money could buy.

ANNE. Mrs. Van Daan, did you have a lot of boy friends before you were married?

MRS. FRANK. (*Coming down again.*) Anne, that's a personal question. It's not courteous to ask personal questions.

MRS. VAN DAAN. Oh, I don't mind. (*To Anne, as Mrs. Frank returns to her duties.*) Our house was always swarming with boys. When I was a girl we had . . .

MR. VAN DAAN. (*Above* R. *end of* C. *table.*) Oh, God. Not again!

MRS. VAN DAAN. (*Good humored.*) Shut up! (*Without a pause, to Anne. Mr. Van Daan mimics Mrs. Van Daan, speaking the first*

29

few words in unison with her, as he paces D. R., *then* L. *below, and* U. L. *again.*) One summer we had a big house in Hilversum. The boys came buzzing around like bees around a jam pot. And when I was sixteen! . . . we were wearing our skirts very short those days and I had good looking legs. (*Crossing to slightly* L. *and below* Mr. Frank. *She is very flirtatious.*) I still have 'em. I may not be as pretty as I used to be, but I still have my legs. (*She pulls up her skirt to above her knees.* Mr. Frank *is a bit non-plussed as he looks up and sees her.*) How about it, Mr. Frank?

MR. VAN DAAN. (*Above* C. *table.*) All right. All right. We see them.

MRS. VAN DAAN. I'm not asking you. I'm asking Mr. Frank.

PETER. Mother, for heaven's sake.

MRS. VAN DAAN. Oh, I embarrass you, do I? (*She crosses back toward Anne at the sofa giving Peter a pat as she passes.*) Well, I just hope the girl you marry has as good. (*Then to Anne.*) My father used to worry about me, with so many boys hanging round. He told me, if any of them gets fresh, you say to him . . . (*She places one hand on Anne's shoulder and with the other holds up a warning finger.* Mr. Van Daan *moves to* D. L., *listening to this.*) "Remember, Mr. So-and-So, remember I'm a lady." (*Gives Anne a little tap on the cheek.*)

ANNE. (*Imitating the action and delivery of* Mrs. Van Daan.) "Remember, Mr. So-and-So, remember I'm a lady." (Mrs. Van Daan *takes the coat from Anne. Anne goes immediately to* D. C. *and sprawls on her stomach on the floor. Head* L., *feet* R., *legs spread wide as she listens for sounds below with an ear pressed to the boards.*)

MR. VAN DAAN. (*During this to* Mrs. Van Daan.) Look at you, talking that way in front of her! Don't you know she puts it all down in that diary?

MRS. VAN DAAN. So if she does? I'm only telling the truth!

MRS. FRANK. (*Coming down to above* C. *table with table cloth she has just taken from* L. *shelves.* Margot *takes all books from her father and puts them on the mantel, then goes to shelves, getting seven plates for her mother.*) Would you mind, Peter, if I moved you over to the couch?

ANNE. (*Listening.*) Miep must have the radio on. (*Peter rises to move to the sofa.* Mr. Van Daan *has moved across above the table and confronts him.*)

30

MR. VAN DAAN. (*To Peter.*) Haven't you finished yet?

PETER. No.

MR. VAN DAAN. You ought to be ashamed of yourself. (*Fade planes. Mr. Van Daan paces L., below the table. He is irritated when he has to step over one of Anne's widespread legs.*)

PETER. All right. All right. I'm a dunce. I'm a hopeless case. Why do I go on? (*Sits on sofa upstage of Mrs. Van Daan. Margot brings plates to Mrs. Frank who has spread the tablecloth, then returns to get knives and forks.*)

MRS. VAN DAAN. (*To Peter.*) You're not hopeless. Don't talk that way. It's just that you haven't anyone to help you, like the girls have. (*To Mr. Frank.*) Maybe you could help him, Mr. Frank?

MR. FRANK. I'm sure that his father . . . ?

MR. VAN DAAN. (*He has continued his circular path to above R. end of C. table.*) Not me. I can't do anything with him. He won't listen to me. You go ahead . . . if you want.

MR. FRANK. What about it, Peter? Shall we make our school co-educational? (*He crosses below table as he speaks, stepping over Anne's upstage leg. Mr. Van Daan strides across her lower leg as he moves L.*)

MRS. VAN DAAN. (*Rising as Mr. Frank comes to her L., she moves below him as she speaks, ending on his L. Margot begins putting knives and forks at the place settings.*) You're an angel, Mr. Frank! An angel! (*She takes Mr. Frank's face in her hands and kisses him on his mouth.*) I don't know why I didn't meet you before I met that one there. (*Indicating Mr. Van Daan who has been watching from L.*) Here, sit down, Mr. Frank. (*Peter moves downstage as Mrs. Van Daan pushes Mr. Frank down on the sofa. She sits above them with her arm over Mr. Frank's shoulder.*) Now, Peter, you listen to Mr. Frank.

MR. FRANK. (*Uncomfortable.*) It might be better for us to go into Peter's room. (*Peter jumps up eagerly, leading the way.*)

MRS. VAN DAAN. That's right. You go in there, Peter. You listen to Mr. Frank. Mr. Frank is a highly educated man. (*Mrs. Frank has been watching all this as she works above the table. Mr. Frank follows close on Peter's heels. She intercepts him as he reaches the L. door, and wipes the lipstick from his lips. Embarrassed, he hurries into Peter's room. During the following scene he and Peter sit on the bed and Mr. Frank helps Peter with his lessons.*)

31

Mr. Van Daan has moved across above the table, swung down R., and across to D. L., stepping again over Anne.)

ANNE. *(On the floor, listening.)* Shh! I can hear a man's voice talking.

MR. VAN DAAN. *(To Anne.)* Isn't it bad enough here without your sprawling all over the place? *(Anne scrambles to a sitting position, her back against the C. table.)*

MRS. VAN DAAN. *(To Mr. Van Daan.)* If you didn't smoke so much, you wouldn't be so bad tempered.

MR. VAN DAAN. Am I smoking? Do you see me smoking?

MRS. VAN DAAN. *(On her feet now, she paces up and down R. C. as the words get hotter.)* Don't tell me you've used up all those cigarettes.

MR. VAN DAAN. One package! Miep only brought me one package!

MRS. VAN DAAN. *(Overlapping.)* It's a filthy habit anyway. It's a good time to break yourself.

MR. VAN DAAN. *(More heated.)* Oh, stop it, please!

MRS. VAN DAAN. You're smoking up all our money. You know that, don't you?

MR. VAN DAAN. *(Shouting her down.)* Will you shut up? *(During this, Mrs. Frank and Margot have studiously kept their eyes down. But Anne, seated on the floor, has been following the discussion interestedly. Mr. Van Daan turns to see her staring up at him.)* And what are you staring at? *(Warn L 84. Anne lamp—Margot.)*

ANNE. I never heard grownups quarrel before. I thought only children quarreled.

MR. VAN DAAN. This isn't a quarrel! It's a discussion. *(He turns away, then back for a final shot.)* And I never heard children so rude before.

ANNE. *(Rising, indignantly.)* I, rude! *(She pursues him L. Margot comes down with spoons and places them around the table.)*

MRS. FRANK. *(Quickly as she sits above the table.)* Anne, will you bring me my knitting? *(Anne goes to get it.)* I must remember, when Miep comes, to ask her to bring me some more wool.

MARGOT. *(Going to Right room.)* I need some hair pins and some soap. I made a list. *(She goes into Right bedroom, turns on the lamp and writes out her list at the dressing table. Site 1 84. Anne lamp—Margot.)*

MRS. FRANK. (*To Anne.*) Have you some library books for Miep when she comes?

ANNE. (*As she brings knitting to her mother.*) It's a wonder that Miep has a life of her own the way we make her run errands for us. Please, Miep, get me some starch. (*Addresses Mr. Van Daan, U. C.*) Please take my hair out and have it cut. Tell me all the latest news, Miep. (*She kneels on the couch above Mrs. Van Daan.*) Did you know she was engaged? His name is Dirk and Miep's afraid the Nazis will ship him off to Germany to work in one of their war plants. That's what they're doing with some of the young Dutchmen . . . they pick them up off the streets ——

MR. VAN DAAN. (*Irriated, he comes to her L. as she rattles on.*) Don't you ever get tired of talking? Suppose you try keeping still for five minutes. Just five minutes. (*He slaps back of hand into palm to emphasize his point, and paces away L. in another swing around the table. Anne clamps her lips tight and strides behind him, mimicking him. As she passes Mrs. Frank, Mrs. Frank jumps up, takes her by the arm and detours her to the sink.*)

MRS. FRANK. Come here, Anne. Finish your glass of milk. (*Mr. Van Daan walks rapidly down around the table again, ending U. L. looking over the shelves. Mrs. Frank gives milk to Anne, then sits C. to knit again.*)

MR. VAN DAAN. (*As he walks.*) Talk, talk, talk. I never heard such a child. Where is my . . . Every evening it's the same, talk, talk, talk. (*He looks around.*) Where the . . . ?

MRS. VAN DAAN. What're you looking for?

MR. VAN DAAN. (*Coming to C.*) My pipe. Have you seen my pipe?

MRS. VAN DAAN. What good's a pipe? You haven't got any tobacco.

MR. VAN DAAN. At least I'll have something to hold in my mouth! (*Opens door R., sticks his head in.*) Margot, have you seen my pipe? (*Anne steals behind his back down to the lamp table, places glass of milk on it and snatches up his pipe from the under shelf. Then she retreats to U. R. C., lips still clamped, hiding pipe behind her back.*)

MARGOT. It was on the table last night.

MR. VAN DAAN. I know. I know. (*Slams door shut, turns to look on mantel.*) Anne, did you see my pipe? (*No answer. He turns slowly to her.*) Anne!

33

MRS. FRANK. Anne, dear, Mr. Van Daan is speaking to you.

ANNE. (*Feigned surprise, through tight lips.*) Am I allowed to talk now?

MR. VAN DAAN. You're the most aggravating . . . (*He controls himself with difficulty.*) The trouble with you is, you've been spoiled. What you need is a good old-fashioned spanking.

ANNE. (*Mimicking Mrs. Van Daan.*) "Remember, Mr. So-and-So, remember I'm a lady." (*She thrusts the pipe into his mouth, then picks up her glass of milk, and crosses to* D. L. C. *Margot enters with list and places it on lamp table, then goes up to the kitchen.*)

MR. VAN DAAN. (*To Anne.*) Why aren't you nice and quiet like your sister Margot? Why do you have to show off all the time? (*Anne darts* R. *trying to get around him but he retreats, blocking her. He ends* R. *of table. She is below and slightly* L. *of him facing up.*) Let me give you a little advice, young lady. Men don't like that kind of thing in a girl. You know that? A man likes a girl who'll listen to him once in a while . . . a domestic girl, who'll keep her house shining for her husband . . . who loves to cook and sew and . . .

ANNE. I'd cut my throat first! I'd open my veins! (*Mr. Van Daan moves toward* U. L.) I'm going to be remarkable! I'm going to Paris . . .

MR. VAN DAAN. (*Derisive.*) Paris . . . !

ANNE. . . . to study music and art.

MR. VAN DAAN. Yeah . . . yeah . . .

ANNE. I'm going to be a famous dancer or singer . . . or something wonderful. (*Arms held wide, milk in right hand, she makes a dancer's turn. The milk spills over the fur coat in Mrs. Van Daan's lap. Mrs. Van Daan is shocked, stunned. Anne falls to her knees, trying to brush the milk away. Margot hurries down to them with a wiping cloth.*)

MRS. VAN DAAN. (*She can scarcely speak.*) Now look what you've done! . . . you clumsy little fool! My beautiful fur coat my father gave me!

ANNE. I'm so sorry.

MRS. VAN DAAN. What do you care? It isn't yours. . . . So go on, ruin it! Do you know what that coat cost? Do you? And now look at it! Look at it!

ANNE. I'm very, very sorry.

MRS. VAN DAAN. (*She crosses* L. *below, then up to the stairs.*) I could kill you for this. I could just kill you! (*Mrs. Van Daan goes up the stairs, clutching the coat. Mr. Van Daan starts after her.*)

MR. VAN DAAN. Petronella . . . liefje! . . . Come back . . . the supper . . come back!

MRS FRANK. (*When they have gone.*) Anne, you mustn't behave in that way. (*Warn* L 85. *Attic on. Margot returns to the sink, taking the glass with her.*)

ANNE. (*Still kneeling.*) It was an accident. Anyone can have an accident.

MRS. FRANK. I don't mean that. I mean the answering back. You must not answer back. (*Anne gets up and moves across above her mother to* L. *She walks heel-to-toe along a crack in the floor, moving to* D. L.) They are our guests. We must always show the greatest courtesy to them. We're all living under terrible tension. That's why we must control ourselves. . . . You don't hear Margot getting into arguments with them, do you? Watch Margot. She's always courteous with them. Never familiar. She keeps her distance. And they respect her for it. Try to be like Margot.

ANNE. (*Turns and starts upstage again.*) And have them walk all over me, the way they do her? No, thanks! (*L* 85.)

MRS. FRANK. I'm not afraid that anyone is going to walk all over you, Anne. I'm afraid for other people, that you'll walk on them. I don't know what happens to you, Anne. You are wild, self-willed. If I had ever talked to my mother as you talk to me . . .

ANNE. Things have changed. People aren't like that any more. "Yes, Mother." "No, Mother." "Anything you say, Mother." I've got to fight things out for myself! Make something of myself!

MRS. FRANK. (*As Anne turns away upstage.*) It isn't necessary to fight to do it. Margot doesn't fight, and isn't she . . . ?

ANNE. (*Violently rebellious, she wheels on her mother.*) Margot! Margot! Margot! Margot! That's all I hear from everyone . . . how wonderful Margot is. . . . "Why aren't you like Margot?"

MARGOT. (*Protesting, comes to* U. C.) Oh, come on, Anne, don't be so . . .

ANNE. (*Paying no attention.*) Everything she does is right, and everything I do is wrong! I'm the goat around here! . . . You're all against me . . . and you worst of all! (*She rushes off into the Right room, and throws herself down on the settee, stifling her* sobs. *Mrs. Frank sighs and crosses to put her knitting on the mantel.*)

MRS. FRANK. (*To Margot.*) Let's put the soup on the stove . . . if there's anyone who cares to eat. Margot, will you take the bread out? (*Margot gets the bread from the cupboard. Mrs. Frank's agitation carries her L.*) I don't know how we can go on living this way. . . . I can't say a word to Anne . . . she flies at me . . .

MARGOT. (*Crossing to shelves for bread plate.*) You know Anne. In half an hour she'll be out here, laughing and joking. (*Warn L 86. Attic off.*)

MRS. FRANK. (*Pacing to C. then D. R.*) And . . . (*She makes a motion upwards, indicating the Van Daans.*) I told your father it wouldn't work . . . but no . . . no . . . he had to ask them, he said . . . he owed it to him, he said. Well, he knows now that I was right! These quarrels . . . this bickering . . .

MARGOT. (*With a warning look, as she places bread on table.*) Shush. Shush. (*The buzzer for the door sounds. Mrs. Frank gasps, startled. The buzzer signal used by Miep and Mr. Kraler is always the International Code "V." Dit-dit-dit-dah.*)

MRS. FRANK. Every time I hear that sound my heart stops!

MARGOT. (*Starting for Peter's door.*) It's Miep. (*She knocks at the door.*) Father? (*L 86. Attic off. Mr. Frank comes quickly from Peter's room and hurries down the steps toward the door leading out.*)

MR. FRANK. (*As he goes.*) Thank you, Margot. Has everyone his list?

MARGOT. I'll get my books. (*To Mrs. Frank, indicating the list on lamp table.*) Here's your list. (*Mrs. Frank goes to lamp table. Margot goes into Right bedroom. Anne sits up, hiding her tears, as Margot comes in.*) Miep's here. (*Margot picks up her books and goes back. Anne goes over to the mirror, smoothing her hair.*)

MR. VAN DAAN. (*Coming down the stairs.*) Is it Miep?

MARGOT. Yes. Father's gone down to let her in.

MR. VAN DAAN. (C. *above table.*) At last I'll have some cigarettes!

MRS. FRANK. (*Coming to him.*) I can't tell you how unhappy I am about Mrs. Van Daan's coat. Anne should never have touched it.

MR. VAN DAAN. She'll be all right.

MRS. FRANK. Is there anything I can do?

36

MR. VAN DAAN. Don't worry. (*He turns to meet Miep. But it is not Miep who comes up the steps. It is Mr. Kraler, followed by Mr. Frank. Their faces are grave. Anne comes from the bedroom. Peter comes from his room.*)

MRS. FRANK. (*As she goes* R. *to below table, meeting him* C.) Mr. Kraler! (*Sound Cue 12 A. Street car.*)

MR. VAN DAAN. (*Shaking his hand across the table.*) How are you, Mr. Kraler?

MARGOT. This is a surprise.

MRS. FRANK. When Mr. Kraler comes the sun begins to shine.

MR. VAN DAAN. Miep is coming?

MR. KRALER. Not tonight. (*Mr. Van Daan moves* U. C. *in disgust. Margot puts books on* R. *end of table.*)

MRS. FRANK. (*To Mr. Kraler.*) Wouldn't you like a cup of coffee? . . . or, better still, will you have supper with us?

MR. KRALER. No, thank you.

MR. FRANK. (D. L.) Mr. Kraler has something to talk over with us. Something has happened, he says, which demands an immediate decision.

MRS. FRANK. (*Fearful.*) What is it? (*As Mr. Kraler talks, he sits down on the couch and opens his briefcase. He takes out bread, cabbages, milk, etc., giving them to Margot and Anne to put in food cabinet. Mrs. Frank sits* R. *of table, Peter stands* L. *of it. Mr. Van Daan takes the chair above the table.*)

MR. KRALER. (U. S. *end couch.*) Usually, when I come up here, I try to bring you some bit of good news. What's the use of telling you the bad news when there's nothing that you can do about it? But today something has happened. . . . Dirk . . . Miep's Dirk, you know, came to me just now. He tells me that he has a Jewish friend living near him. A dentist. He says he's in trouble. He begged me, could I do anything for this man—could I find him a hiding place? . . . So I've come to you. . . . I know it's a terrible thing to ask of you, living as you are, but would you take him in with you?

MR. FRANK. (*Stepping* C.) Of course we will.

MR. KRALER. (*Coming to Mr. Frank.*) It'll be just for a night or two . . . until I find some other place. This happened so suddenly that I didn't know where to turn.

MR. FRANK. Where is he?

MR. KRALER. Downstairs in the office.

37

MR. FRANK. Good. Bring him up.

MR. KRALER. (*Crossing to stairs.*) His name is Dussel . . . Jan Dussel.

MR. FRANK. (*Moving to Kraler.*) Dussel. . . . I think I know him.

MR. KRALER. I'll get him. (*He goes quickly down the steps and out. Mr. Frank suddenly becomes conscious of the others.*)

MR. FRANK. Forgive me. I spoke without consulting you. But I knew you'd feel as I do.

MR. VAN DAAN. There's no reason for you to consult anyone. (*Rises, crosses* D. R.) This is your place. You have a right to do exactly as you please. The only thing I feel . . . there's so little food as it is . . . and to take in another person . . . (*Peter turns away, moving upstage, ashamed of his father.*)

MR. FRANK. We can stretch the food a little. It's only for a few days.

MR. VAN DAAN. You want to make a bet? (*Sits on sofa.*)

MRS. FRANK. I think it's fine to have him. But, Otto, where are you going to put him? Where?

PETER. (*Coming down to above* L. *end of table.*) He can have my bed. I can sleep on the floor. I wouldn't mind.

MR. FRANK. (*Going to Peter.*) That's good of you, Peter. But your room's too small, even for you. (*Peter moves to window. He looks down at men marching by.*) [*Sound Cue 13.*]

ANNE. I have a much better idea. I'll come in here with you and Mother, and Margot can take Peter's room and Peter can go in our room with Mr. Dussel.

MARGOT. (*Above table by her mother.*) That's right. We could do that.

MR. FRANK. No, Margot. You mustn't sleep in that room . . . neither you nor Anne. Mouschi has caught some rats in there. Peter's brave. He doesn't mind.

ANNE. (*Insistent, to Mr. Frank.*) Then how about this? I'll come in here with you and Mother and Mr. Dussel can have my bed.

MRS. FRANK. No! No! Margot will come in here with us and he can have her bed. It's the only way. Margot, bring your things in here. Help her, Anne. (*Margot hurries into Right room to get her things. Peter comes to outside the door to assist.*)

ANNE. (*Rebellious, to her mother.*) Why Margot? Why can't I come in here?

MRS. FRANK. Because it wouldn't be proper for Margot to sleep with a . . . Please, Anne. Don't argue. Please. (*Anne moves over to* R. *door, indignant.*)

MR. FRANK. (*To Anne.*) You don't mind sharing your room with Mr. Dussel, do you, Anne?

ANNE. (*Hiding her hurt.*) No. No, of course not.

MR. FRANK. Good. (*Margot brings robe to Peter. Anne enters Right room and gets nightgown. They bring them into Center room and hang them* U. L. *above shelves. Margot brings a skirt and blouse, then returns for a small box with her comb, brush, jewelry, etc., which she places on shelves. Mrs. Van Daan, having composed herself, starts down the stairs.*) Where's the cognac?

MRS. FRANK. It's there. (*Indicating shelves.*) But, Otto, I was saving it in case of illness.

MR. FRANK. I think we couldn't find a better time to use it. Peter, will you get five glasses for me? (*Peter gets glasses from shelf over sink and puts them on the table, then moves* L. *to his door. Mr. Frank gives Mrs. Frank the bottle and she pours a swallow into each glass. Mrs. Van Daan approaches her husband on the sofa.*)

MRS. VAN DAAN. What's happening? What's going on?

MR. VAN DAAN. (*Sourly.*) Someone's moving in with us.

MRS. VAN DAAN. (*Sits below him on the sofa.*) In here? You're joking.

MARGOT. (*Coming from her room to shelves with her possessions.*) It's only for a night or two . . . until Mr. Kraler finds him another place.

MR. VAN DAAN. Yeah! Yeah! (*Mr. Frank hurries over as Mr. Kraler brings Mr. Dussel up the stairs. Dussel is a man in his fifties, meticulous, finicky . . . bewildered now. He carries a briefcase and shopping bag, stuffed full, and has a small medicine case tucked under his arm. He wears a raincoat and hat.*)

MR. FRANK. (*Hand extended at head of stairs. Anne, all eyes, sits in chair above table.*) Come in, Mr. Dussel.

MR. KRALER. (*Above stairs.*) This is Mr. Frank.

MR. DUSSEL. Mr. Otto Frank?

MR. FRANK. Yes. Let me take your things. (*He takes the hat and bags, handing them to Peter who has come down to above chair* L. *of table. Dussel clings to his medicine case. Peter puts bags under shelves* U. L.) This is my wife Edith . . . and Mrs. Van

Daan, and Mr. Van Daan . . . their son, Peter . . . and my daughters, Margot and Anne. (*Margot and Peter come to above table and Mr. Dussel shakes hands with everyone, crossing* R. *to the Van Daans.*)

MR. KRALER. Thank you, Mr. Frank. Thank you all. Mr. Dussel, I leave you in good hands. Oh . . . Dirk's coat. (*Mr. Kraler moves* D. L., *Dussel hurries to him, taking off the coat. Underneath is his white office jacket, with a yellow Star of David on it.*)

MR. DUSSEL. (*To Mr. Kraler.*) What can I say to thank you . . . ?

MRS. FRANK. (*To Mr. Dussel, as she takes cognac to the Van Daans.*) Mr. Kraler and Miep. . . . They're our life line. Without them we couldn't live.

MR. KRALER. Please. Please. You make us seem very heroic. It isn't that at all. (*Mrs. Frank offers drink to Mr. Kraler. As he refuses, she places it before Mr. Dussel, who has sunk down in chair* L. *of table. Mr. Frank stands above Mr. Dussel. Mr. Kraler moves to* L. *of Mr. Frank as he speaks. Margot goes into her room and straightens beds, sees that all is orderly.*) We simply don't like the Nazis. We don't like their methods. We don't like anything about them.

MR. FRANK. (*Smiling.*) I know. I know. "No one's going to tell us Dutchmen what to do with our damn Jews!"

MR. KRALER. (*To Mr. Dussel.*) Pay no attention to Mr. Frank. I'll be up tomorrow to see that they're treating you right. (*To Mr. Frank.*) Don't trouble to come down again. Peter will bolt the door after me, won't you, Peter?

PETER. (*He hurries across* L.) Yes, sir.

MR. FRANK. Thank you, Peter. I'll do it.

MR. KRALER. Good night. Good night.

GROUP. Good night, Mr. Kraler. We'll see you tomorrow, etc., etc. (*Mr. Kraler goes out with Mr. Frank. Mr. Dussel has risen with the good-byes.*)

MRS. FRANK. Please, Mr. Dussel, sit down. (*The Van Daans, Mrs. Frank, Anne all sit. Peter circles to* D. L. *and sits on the floor, facing Mr. Dussel.*)

MR. DUSSEL. (*As he sits.*) I'm dreaming. I know it. I can't believe my eyes. Mr. Otto Frank here! (*To Mrs. Frank.*) You're not in Switzerland then? A woman told me. . . . She said she'd gone to your house . . . the door was open, everything was in disorder, dishes in the sink. She said she found a piece of paper in the waste basket with an address scribbled on it . . . an address in Zurich. She said you must have escaped to Zurich. (*Margot brings slippers to* U. L., *then returns for final check of the Right room.*)

ANNE. Father put that there purposely . . . just so people would think that very thing!

MR. DUSSEL. And you've been *here* all this time?

MRS. FRANK. All this time . . . ever since July. (*Margot re-enters and stands above the table* R. *of Anne. Anne speaks to her father as he comes back.*)

ANNE. It worked, Pim . . . the address you left! Mr. Dussel says that people believe we escaped to Switzerland.

MR. FRANK. (*Crossing to above* L. *end of table.*) I'm glad. . . . Let's have a little drink to welcome Mr. Dussel. (*All of the grown-ups except Mr. Dussel rise as Mr. Frank lifts his glass and begins his welcoming toast. He breaks off as Mr. Dussel bolts his drink. All are amused. Mr. Frank begins again.*) To Mr. Dussel. Welcome. We're very honored to have you with us.

MRS. FRANK. To Mr. Dussel, welcome. (*The Van Daans murmur a welcome. The "grownups" drink. Mr. Dussel is embarrassed as he realizes he has bolted his drink ahead of time. Anne panto-mimes drinking a big drink.*)

MRS. VAN DAAN. Um. That was good. (*She sits. Mrs. Frank gives Margot a taste. Margot doesn't like it.*)

MR. VAN DAAN. (*To Mr. Dussel.*) Did Mr. Kraler warn you that you won't get much to eat here? You can imagine . . . three ration books among the seven of us . . . and now you make eight. (*Mrs. Van Daan tugs at her husband's coattails. Peter, humiliated, moves* U. L.)

MR. DUSSEL. Mr. Van Daan, you don't realize what is happening outside that you should warn me of a thing like that. You don't realize what's going on. . . . (*Mr. Van Daan puts his glass on the lamp table and resumes his characteristic pacing upstage. Mr. Dussel continues to the others.*) Right here in Amsterdam every day hundreds of Jews disappear. . . . They surround a block and search house by house. Children come back from school to find their parents gone. Hundreds are being deported . . . people that you and I know . . . the Hallensteins . . . the Wessels

MRS. FRANK. (*In tears.*) Oh, no. No!

MR. DUSSEL. (*Crosses to C. of table.*) They get their call-up notice . . . come to the Jewish theatre on such and such a day and hour . . . bring only what you can carry in a rucksack. (*To sofa.*) And if you refuse the call-up notice, then they·come and drag you from your home and ship you off to Mauthausen. The death camp!

MRS. FRANK. We didn't know that things had got so much worse.

MR. DUSSEL. (*Sits upstage of Mrs. Van Daan.*) Forgive me for speaking so.

ANNE. (*Coming to Mr. Dussel.*) Do you know the DeWaals? Do you know what has become of them? Their daughter Jopie and I were in the same class. Jopie's my best friend.

MR. DUSSEL. They are gone.

ANNE. Gone?

MR. DUSSEL. With all the others.

ANNE. Oh, no. Not Jopie! (*She moves upstage in tears. Margot puts her arm comfortingly around her.*)

MRS. VAN DAAN. There were some people called Wagner. They lived near us . . . ?

MR. FRANK. (*Interrupting, with a glance at Anne, he comes to below the table.*) I think we should put this off until later. We all have many questions we want to ask. . . . But I'm sure that Mr. Dussel would like to get settled before supper. (*Peter gets Mr. Dussel's things, hands them across the table to Mr. Frank.*)

MR. DUSSEL. (*Rises, crosses C.*) Thank you. I would. I brought very little with me.

MR. FRANK. (*Giving him his hat and bags. Warn L 9. Anne bracket on—Anne.*) I'm sorry we can't give you a room alone. But I hope you won't be too uncomfortable. We've had to make strict rules here . . . a schedule of hours. . . . We'll tell you after supper. Anne, would you like to take Mr. Dussel to his room? (*He moves around L. end of table, then crosses to Anne. Mr. Dussel takes a few steps after him then turns back.*)

ANNE. (*Controlling her tears.*) If you'll come with me, Mr. Dussel? (*She starts for the Right room.*)

MR. DUSSEL. (*Crosses below to Mrs. Van Daan. Shakes her hand.*) Forgive me if I haven't really expressed my gratitude to all of you. (*Shakes hands with Mrs. Frank, then moves slowly*

42

L. *below and up to Peter, L. Shakes his hand.*) This has been such a shock to me. I'd always thought of myself as Dutch. I was born in Holland. My father was born in Holland, and my grandfather. (*To Margot.*) And now . . . after all these years . . . (*He breaks off.*) If you'll excuse me. (*He shakes hands with Van Daan u. R. C. then Mr. Frank, and follows Anne into the Right room. Site L 9. Anne bracket on—Anne.*)

ANNE. (*Turning on the light.*) Well, here we are. (*Mr. Dussel looks around the room. Anne closes the door. In the Center room Mr. Frank places a comforting hand on Mrs. Frank's shoulder. Margot picks up cognac bottle.*)

MARGOT. The news sounds pretty bad, doesn't it? It's so different from what Mr. Kraler tells us. Mr. Kraler says things are improving.

MR. VAN DAAN. I like it better the way Kraler tells it. (*During the following scene, Margot returns cognac to shelf, then collects glasses and takes them to the sink and rinses and dries them. The Van Daans go upstairs, Peter to his room. Mr. Frank sits in chair above stairwell. Mrs. Frank goes up to the kitchen, gets a bread basket and crosses to him. He takes it and exits U. R. above kitchen. She gets an iron from shelves and follows him off. In Anne's room, Anne turns to Mr. Dussel, who is C., she L.*)

ANNE. You're going to share the room with me.

MR. DUSSEL. I'm a man who's always lived alone. I haven't had to adjust myself to others. I hope you'll bear with me until I learn.

ANNE. Let me help you. (*Places bags on cot R.*) Do you always live all alone? Have you no family at all?

MR. DUSSEL. No one. (*He opens his medicine case and spreads his bottles on the dressing table.*)

ANNE. How dreadful. You must be terribly lonely.

MR. DUSSEL. I'm used to it. (*In his bedroom Peter has taken his cat from the case and holds him up so he can look out the skylight.*)

ANNE. I don't think I could ever get used to it. Didn't you even have a pet? A cat, or a dog?

MR. DUSSEL. I have an allergy for fur-bearing animals. They give me asthma.

ANNE. Oh, dear. Peter has a cat. (*Warn change curtain light on L 10 S 17.*)

MR. DUSSEL.. Here? (*The very thought makes him choke up.*) He has it here?

ANNE. Yes. But we hardly ever see it. He keeps it in his room all the time. I'm sure it will be all right.

MR. DUSSEL. Let us hope so. (*He hastily sips some medicine from one of his bottles.*)

ANNE. That's Margot's bed, where you're going to sleep. I sleep on the sofa there. (*Indicating empty hooks.*) We cleared these off for your things. (*She climbs up on window seat, and peers out. He sits on R. cot to test its softness and is disappointed with it. He tests Anne's sofa and finds it more comfortable.*) The best part about this room . . . you can look down and see a bit of the street and the canal. . . . There's a houseboat . . . you can see the end of it . . . a bargeman lives there with his family. . . . They have a baby and he's just beginning to walk and I'm so afraid he's going to fall into the canal some day. I watch him . . .

MR. DUSSEL. (*Interrupting, as he comes to her.*) Your father spoke of a schedule.

ANNE. Oh, yes. (*She steps down, then urges him to climb up for a look. He does so.*) It's mostly about the times we have to be quiet. And times for the W. C. (*Without any false shame.*) You can use it now if you like.

MR. DUSSEL. (*Stiffly, as he steps down and returns to the table.*) No, thank you.

ANNE. I suppose you think it's awful, my talking about a thing like that. But you don't know how important it can get to be . . . especially when you're frightened. (*He looks at her, appalled at the turn their conversation has taken. As she continues, he takes off his jacket and places it with his bags.*) About this room, the way Margot and I did . . . she had it to herself in the afternoons for studying, reading . . . lessons, you know . . . and I took the mornings. Would that be all right with you?

MR. DUSSEL. (*Removes tie.*) I'm not at my best in the morning.

ANNE. You stay here in the morning then. I'll take the room in the afternoon.

MR. DUSSEL. Tell me, when you're in here, what happens to me? Where am I spending my time? In there, with all the people?

ANNE. Yes.

MR. DUSSEL. I see. I see.

ANNE. We have supper at half past six.

MR. DUSSEL. (*As he goes to the bed* D. C. *and lies down on it, facing front.*) Then, if you don't mind . . . I like to lie down quietly for ten minutes before eating. I find it helps the digestion.

ANNE. Of course. (*Wonders if she should tell him he is on the wrong bed. Decides not to. She comes and bends over him.*) I hope I'm not going to be too much of a bother to you. I seem to be able to get everyone's back up.

MR. DUSSEL. (*Complacent.*) I always get along very well with children. My patients all bring their children to me, because they know I get on well with them. So don't you worry about that. (*He closes his eyes.*)

ANNE. (*She puts out her hand, wanting to shake hands.*) Thank you. Thank you, Mr. Dussel. (*She touches him on the shoulder. He jumps, terrified, and then takes her hand.* 1-2-3-4 *dim. med. fast. As she shakes his hand the scene lights dim quickly, leaving* [*Drop in.*] *them in a lag special, which fades abruptly. The black drop is brought in and Anne's voice comes to us dimly at first,* [*Work light on.*] *and then with increasing power. Curtain light on.*)

ANNE'S VOICE. . . . and yesterday I finished Cissy Van Marx-velt's latest book. I think she is a first-class writer. I shall definitely let my children read her. Monday the twenty-first of September, nineteen forty-two. Mr. Dussel and I had another battle yesterday. Yes, Mr. Dussel! According to him, nothing, I repeat . . . nothing is right about me . . . my appearance, my character, my manners. While he was going on at me I thought . . . sometime I'll give you such a smack that you'll fly right up to the ceiling! Why is it that every grownup thinks he knows the way to bring up children? (*Work light off.*) Particularly the grownups that never had any. I keep wishing Peter was a girl instead of a boy. Then I would have someone to talk to. Margot's a darling, but she takes everything too seriously. (*Drop up. Dim slow. Drop out.*) To pause for a moment on the subject of Mrs. Van Daan. (*Voice begins to fade out. Lights begin to dim up, cyclorama followed by acting area.*) I must tell you that her attempts to flirt with Father are getting her nowhere. Pim, thank goodness, won't play. (*Voice out. Lights full.*)

ACT I

SCENE 4

ON RISE: *Whistles. (Sound Cue 14.) It is the middle of the night, several months later. The stage is dark except for a little light coming through the skylight in Peter's room and the faintest trace of a cool glow, making it possible to distinguish the forms of Anne in her bed and her parents asleep on the couch. Mrs. Frank lies on the seat section, Mr. Frank on the shelf pulled out from the base. His overcoat is thrown over him. Their heads are downstage. Site: Anne's lamp—Dussel 1 12. Margot is asleep* U. L. *by the shelves with the curtain pulled across the foot of her pallet. In the Attic Mrs. Van Daan is asleep. Mr. Van Daan in trousers and undershirt is moving quietly toward the head of the stairs. "Just a Dream": Hanging lamp—Margot L 13. He strikes a match to light his way, but extinguishes it at once as he starts down. Site: Peter's lamp. Peter L 14. From outside we hear two drunken German soldiers singing, "Lili Marlene." (Sound Cue 15.) A girl's high giggle is heard as the trio clumps unsteadily by. As these voices fade away, Mr. Van Daan strikes another match at the foot of the stairs, blows it out, and we hear him open and close the food chest under the sink. "Endangering Our Lives." Attic—Mrs. Van Daan L 15. Outside, we hear running footsteps approach on the cobblestones and pass into the distance. (Sound Cue 16.) Site: Boy Blue lamp—Margot L 16. We see Mr. Van Daan's dim figure sneaking back up the stairs. After a pause we hear the sound of heavy boots again as they run by and fade away down the street. (Sound Cue 17.) Warn L16A. W. C. on. Van Daan is upstairs again and all is quiet. Suddenly out of the silence and dark, we hear Anne scream.*

ANNE. *(Screaming.)* No! No! Don't . . . don't take me! *(She moans, tossing and crying in her sleep. The other people wake, terrified. Mr. Dussel sits up in bed, furious.)*

46

MR. DUSSEL. Shush! Anne! Anne, for God's sake, shush!

ANNE. (*Still in her nightmare.*) Save me! Save me! (*She screams and screams. Mr. Dussel gets out of bed, going over to her, trying to wake her.*)

MR. DUSSEL. For God's sake! Quiet! Quiet! You want someone to hear? (*Mrs. Frank snatches up her shawl and, rushing in to Anne, sits on her bed, taking her in her arms. Mr. Frank hurriedly gets up, putting on his overcoat. Margot sits up terrified, then rushes over to get the footstool. She drags it to u. c. so that she can reach the hanging lamp. Peter puts up his blackout curtain. Planes are heard high overhead.*) [*Sound Cue 18.*]

MRS. FRANK. (*To Anne, in her room.*) Hush, darling, hush. It's all right. There, there . . . my poor baby . . . my child. (*Over her shoulder to Dussel, who is blowing his nose.*) Will you be kind enough to turn on the light, Mr. Dussel? (*He does so. Wall bracket.*) It's nothing, my darling. It was just a dream. (*Margot turns on the hanging lamp in the Center room. Gradually Anne comes out of her nightmare, still trembling with horror. Mr. Frank has come into her room and goes to peer out past the blackout curtain over the window. He must be sure that no one in the street has heard the screams. Peter turns on the light in his room, slips into his robe and comes into the Center room on his way to Anne's door.*)

MR. DUSSEL. (*To Mrs. Frank.*) Something must be done about that child, Mrs. Frank. Yelling like that! Who knows but there's somebody on the street? She's endangering all our lives. (*Mr. Van Daan turns on the Attic light and starts down. Margot pulls on her robe and crosses down to the lamp table where she lights the lamp.*)

MRS. FRANK. Anne, darling. Little Anne.

MR. DUSSEL. Every night she twists and turns. I don't sleep. I spend half my night shushing her. And now it's nightmares! (*Margot comes to the door of Anne's room, followed by Peter. Mr. Frank goes to them, indicating that everything is all right. Peter takes Margot back to her pallet.*)

MRS. FRANK. (*To Anne.*) You're here, safe, you see? Nothing has happened. (*To Mr. Dussel.*) Please, Mr. Dussel, go back to bed. She'll be herself in a minute or two. Won't you, Anne?

MR. DUSSEL. (*Gets his glasses, pillow and book from the chest.*) Thank you, but I'm going to the W. C. The one place where there's

47

peace! (*He stalks out. Mr. Van Daan, still in underwear and trousers, comes down the stairs to* U. C.)

MR. VAN DAAN. What is it? What happened?

MR. DUSSEL. A nightmare. She was having a nightmare!

MR. VAN DAAN. I thought someone was murdering her.

MR. DUSSEL. Unfortunately, no. (*He goes into the bathroom. Mr. Van Daan goes back up the stairs, explaining all to his wife who waits fearfully. Mr. Frank comes into the Center room.*)

MR. FRANK. Thank you, Peter. Go back to bed. (*Peter goes back to his room. Mr. Frank follows him, turning out the light and looking out of the window. Site L17. Peter's lamp—Frank. Then he goes back to the Center room, and gets up on the stool, turning off the* C. *hanging lamp. Peter takes down his blackout curtain, looks for planes a while, then lies down on his bed in his dark robe. Margot sits on her bed. Site L18. Hanging lamp—Frank.*)

MRS. FRANK. (*To Anne, through the above action.*) Would you like some water? (*Anne shakes her head.*) Was it a very bad dream? Perhaps if you told me . . . ?

ANNE. I'd rather not talk about it.

MRS. FRANK. Poor darling. Try to sleep then. I'll sit right here beside you until you fall asleep. (*She brings the stool from the dressing table to Anne's bed.*)

ANNE. You don't have to.

MRS. FRANK. But I'd like to stay with you . . . very much. Really.

ANNE. I'd rather you didn't. (*In the Center room Mr. Frank returns to his bed, stands listening to the planes for a moment, then sits on the upstage end of the bed.*)

MRS. FRANK. Good night, then. (*She leans down to kiss Anne. Anne puts her arm across her face and turns away. Mrs. Frank tries not to show her hurt. She kisses Anne's arm instead.*) You'll be all right? There's nothing that you want?

ANNE. Will you please ask Father to come.

MRS. FRANK. (*After a second.*) Of course, Anne dear. (*She hurries into the Center room fighting back her tears. Passing Mr. Frank, she ends* C., *below the table. In the Attic, Mr. Van Daan turns off the light and they settle down. L 19. Attic off. The planes fade away in the distance.*) She wants you.

MR. FRANK. (*Sensing her hurt, he goes to her.*) Edith, dear!

MRS. FRANK. It's all right. I thank God that at least she will

48

turn to you when she needs comfort. Go to her, Otto. She is still shaking with fear. (*As Mr. Frank hesitates.*) Go to her. (*Mr. Frank looks at Mrs. Frank for a second as she moves toward the bed. Then he crosses L. and up to the shelves. He gets a pill from a bottle there and a cup. He goes to the sink for water. Mrs. Frank sits on the foot of her bed trying to keep from sobbing aloud. Margot comes to her, sits by her and puts her arms around her.*) She wants nothing of me. She pulled away when I leaned down to kiss her.

MARGOT. It's a phase. . . . You heard Father. . . . Most girls go through it . . . they turn to their fathers at this age . . . they give all their love to their fathers.

MRS. FRANK. You weren't like this. You didn't shut me out.

MARGOT. She'll get over it. (*Mr. Frank enters Anne's room, pulls the stool aside and places the cup on it. As he goes to Anne she sits up and flings her arms around him, clinging to him. In the Center room Margot takes the shawl from her mother, smooths the bed, and Mrs. Frank lies down. Margot sits beside her a moment, comforting her.*)

ANNE. (*During this—to Mr. Frank.*) Oh, Pim. I dreamed that they came to get us! The Green Police! They broke down the door and grabbed me and started to drag me out the way they did Jopie.

MR. FRANK. I want you to take this pill.

ANNE. What is it?

MR. FRANK. (*Give standby for L21. As Margot rises.*) Something to quiet you. (*She takes it and drinks the water.*) Do you want me to read to you for a while?

ANNE. No. Just sit with me for a minute. (*He sits on the edge of the bed beside her, replaces cup on stool.*) Was I awful? Did I yell terribly loud? Do you think anyone outside could have heard? (*Margot turns off the lamp in the Center room and goes back to her bed.*)

MR. FRANK. (*Site L21. Boy Blue off—Margot.*) No. No. Lie quietly now. Try to sleep.

ANNE. (*She lies back, still overwrought.*) I'm a terrible coward. I'm so disappointed in myself. I think I've conquered my fear . . . I think I'm really grown up . . . and then something happens . . . and I run to you like a baby. . . . I love you, Father. I don't love anyone but you.

MR. FRANK. (*Reproachfully.*) Anneline!

ANNE. (*Pushing herself up on her elbows.*) It's true. I've been thinking about it for a long time. You're the only one I love.

MR. FRANK. It's fine to hear you tell me that you love me. But I'd be much happier if you said you loved your mother as well. . . . She needs your help so much . . . your love . . .

ANNE. We have nothing in common. She doesn't understand me. Whenever I try to explain my views on life to her she asks me if I'm constipated. (*She falls back. Warn change L22 S21.*)

MR. FRANK. You hurt her very much just now. She's crying. She's in there crying. (*Curtain light on.*)

ANNE. I can't help it. I only told the truth. I didn't want her here. . . . (*Then, with sudden remorse, she sits up and clings to him again.*) Oh, Pim, I was horrible, wasn't I? And the worst of it is, I can stand off and look at myself doing it and know it's cruel and yet I can't stop doing it. What's the matter with me? Tell me. Don't say it's just a phase! Help me.

MR. FRANK. There is so little that we parents can do to help our children. We can only try to set a good example . . . point the way. The rest you must do yourself. You must build your own character.

ANNE. I'm trying. Really I am. (*She lies back again more relaxed.*) Every night before I go to sleep I think back over all of the things I did that day that were wrong . . . like putting the wet mop in Mr. Dussel's bed . . . and this thing now with Mother. I say to myself, that was wrong. I make up my mind, I'm never going to do that again. Never! Of course I may do something worse, but at least I'll never do *that* again! (*The medicine begins its work. As she talks she becomes relaxed, drowsy.*) I have a nicer side, Father . . . a sweeter, nicer side. But I'm scared to show it. I'm afraid that people are going to laugh at me if I'm serious. So the mean Anne comes to the outside and the good Anne stays on the inside and I keep on trying to switch them around and have the good Anne outside and the bad Anne inside and be what I'd like to be . . . and might be . . . if only . . . only . . . (*She is asleep. Mr. Frank rises quietly, places the cup on the dressing table and goes to the door. He turns to look at her once more, then turns out the light. Mrs. Frank sits up as he enters the Center room and the scene lights fade slowly as he comes to her. The black drop is brought in and we hear Anne's voice fading slowly in. Site—bumps dim. Drop in. Work light on. Curtain light on.*)

50

ANNE'S VOICE. . . . the air raids are getting worse. They come over day and night. The noise is terrifying. Pim says it should be music to our ears. The more planes, the sooner will come the end of the war. Mrs. Van Daan pretends to be a fatalist. What will be, will be. But when the planes come over, who is the most frightened? No one else but Petronella! . . . Monday, the ninth of November, nineteen forty-two. Wonderful news. The Allies have landed in Africa. Pim says that we can look for an early finish to the war. Just for fun he asked each of us what was the first thing we wanted to do when we got out of here. Mrs. Van Daan longs to be home with her own things, her needlepoint chairs, the Beckstein piano her father gave her . . . the best that money could buy. Peter would like to go to a movie. Mr. Dussel wants to get back to his dentist's drill. He's afraid he is losing his touch. For myself, there are so many things . . . to ride a bike again . . . to laugh till my belly aches . . . to have new clothes from the skin out. . . . (*Work light off. Drop out. Scene lights begin to fade in. Voice begins to fade out.*) . . . to have a hot tub filled to overflowing and wallow in it for hours . . . to be back in school with my friends . . . (*Dim slow. Voice out. Lights three-quarters full and rising.*)

ACT I

SCENE 5

Stage L. Weak whistles on rise. [Sound Cue 19.]
SCENE: *It is the first night of the Hanukkah celebration in December of that year, 1942. The C. table, with the lamp table to extend its length, has been placed in front of the couch. A tablecloth covers this and is set with a small bowl of sliced apples and walnuts, a small decanter of wine and a pitcher of water.*
Downstage of the couch Peter sits on the stool from Anne's room. Mrs. Van Daan is on the downstage end of the couch, Mr. Van Daan sits in the center, Mrs. Frank above. Mr. Frank stands at the upstage end of the table. An armchair is at his place. Margot sits in a straight

chair opposite her mother. Dussel sits in an armchair be-
low her and Anne is on the footstool below him. As the
lights fade up Mr. Frank lights the Shamos, or servant
candle on the Menorah before him. He takes it and holds
it up as he reads the blessing from a prayer book. The
"family" are dressed in their best. The men wear hats,
Peter wears his cap. The hanging and mantel lamps are
on, but the lighting is concentrated on the table area,
suggesting a warm candlelight.

MR. FRANK. (*Reading.*) "Praised be Thou, Oh Lord, our God,
Ruler of the universe, who has sanctified us with Thy command-
ments and bidden us kindle the Hanukkah lights. Praised be Thou,
Oh Lord our God, Ruler of the universe, who has wrought won-
drous deliverances for our fathers in days of old. Praised be Thou,
oh Lord, our God, Ruler of the universe, that Thou hast given us
life and sustenance and brought us to this happy season. Amen."
(*Pronounced O-mein. Mr. Frank starts to light the one candle of
the Menorah with the servant candle as he continues.*) We kindle
this Hanukkah light to celebrate the great and wonderful deeds
wrought through the zeal with which God filled the hearts of the
heroic Maccabees, two thousand years ago. They fought against
indifference, against tyranny and oppression, and they restored
our Temple to us. May these lights remind us that we should ever
look to God, whence cometh our help. Amen.
ALL. Amen. (O-mein.) (*Mr. Frank hands Mrs. Frank the prayer
book. He sits as she rises.*)
MRS. FRANK. (*Reading Psalm CXXI.*) "I lift up mine eyes unto
the mountains, from whence cometh my help. My help cometh
from the Lord who made heaven and earth. He will not suffer thy
foot to be moved. He that keepeth thee will not slumber. He that
keepeth Israel doth neither slumber nor sleep. The Lord is thy
keeper. The Lord is thy shade upon thy right hand. The sun shall
not smite thee by day, nor the moon by night. The Lord shall
keep thee from all evil. He shall keep thy soul. The Lord shall
guard thy going out and thy coming in, from this time forth and
forevermore." Amen.
ALL. Amen. (*Mrs. Frank returns the prayerbook to Mr. Frank,
then hurries to the shelves to get eight plates. Margot goes to help
her. She will bring eight glasses.*)

MR. DUSSEL. (*As he rises and hands his hat to Mr. Frank.*) That was very moving.

ANNE. (*Pulling him back.*) It isn't over yet!

MRS. VAN DAAN. Sit down! Sit down! (*Mr. Frank collects Van Daan's and Mr. Dussel's hats and takes them with his own, and the prayerbook to the mantel. He returns and sits again. Peter puts his cap in his pocket. Van Daan starts to eat.*)

ANNE. (*To Dussel.*) There's lots more, songs and presents.

MR. DUSSEL. Presents?

MRS. FRANK. (*As she returns to her place and distributes plates around the table.*) Not this year, unfortunately.

MRS. VAN DAAN. But always on Hanukkah everyone gives presents . . . everyone!

MR. DUSSEL. Like our St. Nicholas' Day. (*There is a chorus of "no's" from the group.*)

MRS. VAN DAAN. No! Not like St. Nicholas! What kind of a Jew are you that you don't know Hanukkah!

MRS. FRANK. (*To Mr. Dussel.*) I remember particularly the candles. . . . First one, as we have tonight. Then the second night you light two candles, then the next night three . . . and so on until you have eight candles burning. When there are eight candles it is truly beautiful. (*Mrs. Frank hurries to the shelves again to get two cups. Margot has returned to just above her, listening to the story. As Mrs. Frank moves away she steps down, placing the glasses on the table. Mr. Dussel pours the wine. Margot returns to her chair. Mrs. Van Daan waters hers and Peter's wine.*)

MRS. VAN DAAN. (*Giving glass to Peter.*) And the potato pancakes. (*Mrs. Frank waters the rest of the glasses of wine.*)

MR. VAN DAAN. Don't talk about them!

MRS. VAN DAAN. I make the best *latkes* you ever tasted!

MRS. FRANK. Invite us all next year . . . in your own home.

MR. FRANK. God willing!

MRS. VAN DAAN. God willing.

MARGOT. (*Standing at her place.*) What I remember best is the presents we used to get when we were little . . . eight days of presents . . . and each day they got better and better.

MRS. FRANK. (*Sitting down.*) We are all here, alive. That is present enough.

ANNE. (*Excitedly.*) No it isn't. I've got something . . . (*She jumps up, rushes toward her room.*)

MRS. FRANK. What is it?

ANNE. Presents! (*She darts into her room, hurriedly puts on a little party hat she has improvised from her lampshade. A paper flower, bits of ribbons cover it. An elastic goes under her chin. She snatches up her school satchel bulging with parcels and comes running back to L. C. She puts the bag on the floor.*)

MRS. VAN DAAN. (*During this.*) Presents!

ALL. (*A toast is led by Mr. Van Daan.*) L'chaim, l'chaim!

MR. DUSSEL. (*On Anne's entrance.*) Look!

MR. VAN DAAN. What's she got on her head?

PETER. A lampshade!

ANNE. (*With the satchel.*) Oh dear. They're every which way. (*She pulls one out at random, a thin book in a manila envelope. She has written a poem on the outside. Anne is breathless with excitement.*) This is for Margot. (*She hands it to Margot, pulling her to her feet. She is between Margot and Mr. Frank.*) Read it out loud.

MARGOT. (*Reading.*)

"You have never lost your temper,
You never will, I fear,
You are so good.
But if you should,
Put all your cross words here."

(*Slips book out of the envelope. Mrs. Frank half rises as she says, "What is it?"*) A new crossword puzzle book! Where did you ever get it?

ANNE. It isn't new. It's one that you've done. But I rubbed it all out and if you wait a little and forget, you can do it all over again. (*Returns to satchel.*)

MARGOT. (*Sitting.*) It's wonderful, Anne. Thank you. You'd never know it wasn't new. (*From outside we hear the sound of a streetcar passing.*) [Sound Cue 20.]

ANNE. (*Coming to between her mother and father with a small bottle half filled with liquid, wrapped in a scrap of paper.*) Mrs. Van Daan.

MRS. VAN DAAN. (*Taking it and opening it.*) This is awful . . . I haven't anything for anyone . . . I never thought . . .

MR. FRANK. This is all Anne's idea.

MRS. VAN DAAN. (*Holding up the bottle.*) What is it?

ANNE. It's hair shampoo. I took all the odds and ends of soap and mixed them with the last of my toilet water.

MRS. VAN DAAN. Oh, Anneke! (*She takes off the top, sniffs, then lets the others smell.*)

ANNE. (*Returns to satchel.*) I wanted to write a poem for all of them, but I didn't have time. (*She takes out a shoebox, hides it behind her, and imitates Mr. Van Daan's walk and voice as she returns to R. of Mr. Frank.*) Yours, Mr. Van Daan, is *really* something . . . something you want more than anything. (*As she waits for him to open it.*) Look! Cigarettes!

MR. VAN DAAN. (*Delighted, he pulls out two dark brown cigarettes.*) Cigarettes!

ANNE. Two of them! Pim found some old pipe tobacco in the pocket lining of his coat . . . and we made them . . . or rather, Pim did.

MRS. VAN DAAN. Let me see. . . . Well, look at that! Light it, Putti! Light it. (*Mr. Van Daan hesitates, cigarette in hand, looking suspiciously at Anne.*)

ANNE. (*Reassuring him.*) It's tobacco, really it is! There's a little fluff in it, but not much. (*Everyone watches intently as Mr. Van Daan cautiously lights it.*)

PETER. It works!

MR. VAN DAAN. Look at him. (*The cigarette flares up. Everyone laughs as Mr. Van Daan coughs and chokes.*)

MR. VAN DAAN. (*Spluttering.*) Thank you, Anne. Thank you. (*Anne rushes back to her satchel for another present.*)

ANNE. (*Handing Mrs. Frank a piece of paper.*) For Mother, Hanukkah greeting. (*She pulls Mrs. Frank to her feet.*)

MRS. FRANK. (*Reading.*)

"Here's an I.O.U. that I promise to pay.
Ten hours of doing whatever you say. Signed, Anne Frank."

(*Mrs. Frank, touched, takes Anne in her arms, holding her close.*)

MR. DUSSEL. (*To Anne.*) Ten hours of doing what you're told? *Anything* you're told?

ANNE. That's right. (*She returns to satchel.*)

MR. DUSSEL. (*After thinking it over for a second.*) You wouldn't want to sell that, Mrs. Frank?

MRS. FRANK. Never! This is the most precious gift I've ever had! (*She sits showing the piece of paper to the others. Anne pulls out a scarf, the same scarf we saw in the first scene. She comes to L. of Mr. Frank.)

ANNE. For Pim.

MR. FRANK. Anneke . . . I wasn't supposed to have a present! (He takes it, unfolding it and showing it to the others. He puts it on, tucking it inside his jacket.)

ANNE. It's a muffler . . . to put around your neck . . . like an Ascot, you know. I made it myself out of odds and ends. . . . I knitted it in the dark each night, after I'd gone to bed. (Ruefully.) I'm afraid it looks better in the dark! (She gets Peter's and Mouschi's presents, then returns to Mr. Frank's left.)

MR. FRANK. It's fine. It fits me perfectly. Thank you, Annele.

ANNE. (Going to Peter, handing him a ball of paper with a ribbon and little bells attached to it.) That's for Mouschi.

PETER. (Rising to bow.) On behalf of Mouschi, I thank you. (He sits again.)

ANNE. (Hesitant, handing him a gift.) And . . . this is yours . . . from Mrs. Quack Quack. (He holds the little case gingerly in his hands.) Well . . . open it. . . . Aren't you going to open it? (Impatient, excited, she moves C. behind Mr. Dussel.)

PETER. I'm scared to. I know something's going to jump out and hit me.

ANNE. No. It's nothing like that, really.

MRS. VAN DAAN. (As he is opening it.) What is it, Peter? Go on. Show it.

ANNE. (Excitedly.) It's a safety razor!

MR. DUSSEL. A what?

ANNE. A razor!

MRS. VAN DAAN. (To Anne.) You didn't make that out of odds and ends.

ANNE. (To Peter.) Miep got it for me. It's not new. It's second hand. (To Peter.) But you really do need a razor now.

MR. DUSSEL. (Peering across at Peter.) For what?

ANNE. (Pointing to Peter.) Look on his upper lip . . . you can see the beginning of a moustache.

MR. DUSSEL. He wants to get rid of that? Put a little milk on it and let the cat lick it off.

PETER. (Starting for his room.) Think you're funny, don't you?

MR. DUSSEL. Look! He can't wait! He's going in to try it!

PETER. I'm going in to give Mouschi his present! (He goes into

56

*his room, slamming the door behind him. With his back to the
audience sits on the window seat, rolls up a towel and tucks it into
his jacket.)*

MR. VAN DAAN. (*Disgustedly.*) Mouschi, Mouschi, Mouschi.
(*In the distance we hear a dog persistently barking. [Sound Cue
21.] Anne brings a gift to Mr. Dussel.)*

ANNE. And last but never least, my roommate, Mr. Dussel.

MR. DUSSEL. (*Surprised, he swings his chair so he is facing
nearly front.*) For me? You have something for me? (*Beaming, he
opens the tiny box she gives him.*)

ANNE. I made them myself.

MR. DUSSEL. (*Puzzled.*) Capsules! Two capsules!

ANNE. (*Excitedly.*) They're ear-plugs!

MR. DUSSEL. Ear-plugs?

ANNE. To put in your ears so you won't hear me when I thrash
around at night. I saw them advertised in a magazine. They're not
real ones. . . . I made them out of cotton and candle wax. Try
them. . . . See if they don't work . . . see if you can hear me
talk. . . .

MR. DUSSEL. (*Putting one in his ear.*) Wait now until I get them
in . . . (*Putting the other in.*) so.

ANNE. Are you ready?

MR. DUSSEL. Huh?

ANNE. (*Louder.*) Are you ready?

MR. DUSSEL. (*Rises with an agonized look on his face.*) Good
God! They've gone inside! (*He crosses to L. C. thumping his head,
trying frantically to get out the plugs. Everyone laughs except
Anne, who is chagrined at the turn of events.*) I can't get them
out! (*Finally he gets them out and crosses to above and just R. of
Mr. Frank.*) Thank you, Anne! Thank you! (*Pockets the plugs.*)

THE GROUP. (*Speaking together.*)

| MR. VAN DAAN. A real Hanukkah! | MRS. VAN DAAN. Wasn't it cute of her? |
| MRS. FRANK. I don't know when she did it. | MARGOT. I love my present. |

ANNE. (*Sitting at her place.*) And now let's have the song, Father . . . please. . . . (*To Mr. Dussel.*) Have you heard the
Hanukkah song, Mr. Dussel? The song is the whole thing! (*She
sings enthusiastically.*) "Oh, Hanukkah, Oh, Hannukkah. A sweet
celebration . . ."

57

MR. FRANK. (*Quieting her.*) I'm afraid, Anne, we shouldn't sing that song tonight. (*To Mr. Dussel.*) It's a song of jubilation, of rejoicing. One is apt to become too enthusiastic.

ANNE. Oh, please, please. Let's sing the song. I promise not to shout! (*Peter is coming from his bedroom, ostentatiously holding a bulge in his coat as if he were holding his cat, and dangling Mouschi's present before it.*)

MR. FRANK. (*To Anne.*) Very well. But quietly now. . . . I'll keep an eye on you and when . . .

MR. DUSSEL. (*Pointing to Peter, he begins to wheeze and cough.*) You . . . You! How many times . . . I told you . . . Out! Out!

MR. VAN DAAN. (*Brushing past Mrs. Van Daan he strides to Peter who is standing just above the stairwell.*) What's the matter with you? Haven't you any sense? Get that cat out of here.

PETER. (*Innocently.*) Cat?

MR. VAN DAAN. You heard me. Get it out of here!

PETER. I have no cat. (*Delighted with his joke he pulls the towel from his coat, holding it high for all to see. The group at the table laugh, enjoying the joke. Peter puts ball and towel in shelf area.*)

MR. DUSSEL. (*Still wheezing.*) It doesn't need to be the cat . . . his clothes are enough . . . (*He coughs unconvincingly to prove his point.*) when he comes out of that room . . .

MR. VAN DAAN. (*Going to Mr. Dussel.*) Don't worry. You won't be bothered any more. We're getting rid of it.

MR. DUSSEL. At last you listen to me. (*He goes into Right room. Warn L27-L28. Mantel. Hanging.*)

MR. VAN DAAN. (*Calling after him.*) I'm not doing it for you. That's all in your mind . . . all of it! (*In the Right bedroom Mr. Dussel takes a swallow of his medicine, then sits on his bed to recover. Van Daan goes L. above the table, then circles below, going back to his place.*) I'm doing it because I'm sick of seeing that cat eat all our food.

PETER. (*Crossing to back of Mr. Dussel's chair at the table.*) That's not true! I only give him bones . . . scraps . . .

MR. VAN DAAN. (*Standing at his place.*) Don't tell me! He gets fatter every day! Damn cat looks better than any of us. Out he goes tonight! (*He sits.*)

PETER. No! No!

ANNE. (*Shifting into Mr. Dussel's chair, she defends Peter.*)

Mr. Van Daan, you can't do that! That's Peter's cat. Peter loves that cat.

MRS. FRANK. (*Quietly.*) Anne.

PETER. (*An ultimatum.*) If he goes, I go.

MR. VAN DAAN. (*Unworried.*) Go! Go!

MRS. VAN DAAN. (*Putting a finish to the argument.*) You're not going and the cat's not going! (*Peter moves away* U. L.) Now please . . . this is Hanukkah! . . . Hanukkah! . . . this is the time to celebrate! . . . what's the matter with all of you? Come on, Anne! Let's have the song!

ANNE. (*Spirited, singing.*)

"Oh, Hanukkah. Oh, Hanukkah.

The sweet celebration."

MR. FRANK. (*Rising, stopping her.*) I think we should first blow out the candle . . . (*Margot makes a little sound of protest, he explains further.*) then we'll have something for tomorrow night.

MARGOT. But, Father, you're supposed to let them burn themselves out.

MR. FRANK. I'm sure that God understands shortages. (*Peter comes to behind Margot's chair. Mr. Frank prays.*) "Praised be Thou, oh Lord our God, who hast sustained us and permitted us to celebrate this joyous festival." Amen (*Before he can blow out the candle there is a sudden crash of something falling below. The dog starts to bark again. [Sound Cue 22.] They all freeze in horror, motionless, straining to hear. For a few seconds there is complete silence. Then Mrs. Frank snatches off her shoes and moves swiftly to the mantel, turning off the lamp. Site L27. Mantel Mrs. Frank. As she moves, Mr. Frank hurries to the head of the stairs. Mr. Van Daan follows to just above him. All take off their shoes. Mr. Frank signals Peter to turn off the C. lamp. Mrs. Frank crosses above to* U. L. C. *Site L28. Hanging lamp—Peter. Peter cannot reach the chain so he pulls the chair from* U. R. *to position under the lamp. He stands on it. Just as he is touching the lamp he loses his balance. The chair goes out from under him. He falls. The iron shade crashes to the floor. There is the sound of feet below, running down the stairs. [Sound Cue 23.] Peter picks himself up immediately.*)

MR. VAN DAAN. (*Under his breath, as he goes toward Peter.*) God Almighty! (*Mr. Dussel has come to the door of his room on the crash. He moves toward Peter gesturing for silence. Margot*

59

rises at her place. Anne moves to L. C. *Van Daan moves back to above Mr. Frank, listening. The footsteps die away. The following lines are whispered.*) Do you hear anything?

MR. FRANK. (*Listens carefully for another moment.*) No. I think they've gone.

MRS. VAN DAAN. (*A trace of hysteria in her voice. She is standing* D. R. *of the table.*) It's the Green Police! They've found us!

MR. FRANK. If they had, they wouldn't have left. They'd be up here by now.

MRS. VAN DAAN. I know it's the Green Police! They've gone to get help. That's all. They'll be back!

MR. VAN DAAN. Or it may have been the Gestapo, looking for papers . . .

MR. FRANK. Or a thief, looking for money.

MRS. VAN DAAN. We've got to do something. . . . Quick! Quick! Before they come back.

MR. VAN DAAN. There isn't anything to do. Just wait. (*Mr. Frank holds up his hand for them to be quiet. He is listening intently. There is complete silence as they all strain to hear any sound from below. Suddenly Anne begins to sway. With a low cry she falls to the floor in a faint. Mrs. Frank goes to her quickly. She sits on the floor lifting Anne's head to her lap.*)

MRS. FRANK. Get some water, please. Get some water. (*Margot starts toward the sink.*)

MR. VAN DAAN. (*Grabbing Margot.*) No. No. No one's going to run water!

MR. FRANK. If they've found us, they've found us. Get the water. (*Margot continues to the sink. Mr. Frank goes to the shelves, picks up a flashlight.*) I'm going down. (*Margot rushes to him, clinging to him as he starts for the stairs. Anne struggles back to consciousness.*)

MARGOT. No, Father, no! There may be someone there, waiting. . . . It may be a trap!

MR. FRANK. This is Saturday. There is no way for us to know what has happened until Miep or Mr. Kraler come on Monday morning. We cannot live with this uncertainty.

MARGOT. Don't go, Father! (*Cellar light on.*)

MRS. FRANK. Hush, darling, hush. (*Mr. Frank shakes Margot*

off, slips quietly down the steps and out below.) Margot! Stay close to me. (*Margot goes to her mother.*)

MR. VAN DAAN. (*To Mrs. Frank.*) Shush! Shush! (*Squeezing between Mrs. Frank and the table he crosses to below the end of the couch, passing below Mrs. Van Daan, who has crept toward c. Margot remembers the water for Anne and goes to get it. She will return to kneel L. of Mrs. Frank and give Anne a sip.*)

MRS. VAN DAAN. (*Becoming hysterical.*) Putti, where's our money? Get our money. I hear you can buy the Green Police off, so much a head. Go upstairs, quick! Get the money!

MR. VAN DAAN. Keep still!

MRS. VAN DAAN. (*Pleading.*) Do you want to be dragged off to a concentration camp? Are you going to stand there and wait for them to come up and get you? (*Sinking to her knees before him as her hysteria mounts.*) Do something, I tell you!

MR. VAN DAAN. Will you keep still! (*He shoves her aside as he crosses quietly, quickly to the stairs to listen. She falls sobbing against the sofa. Peter hurries down to her below the table. He helps her to sit on the sofa. There is a second of silence, then Anne can stand it no longer. Warn L29. Mantel—Margot.*)

ANNE. Someone go after Father! Make Father come back! (*Mrs. Frank covers Anne's mouth to muffle her voice.*)

PETER. (*Hurrying L. to the stairwell.*) I'll go.

MR. VAN DAAN. (*He is at the stairs listening. As Peter approaches he turns on him.*) Haven't you done enough? (*He pushes Peter roughly U. L. Peter grabs a chair as if to hit Mr. Van Daan with it. Then puts it down, burying his face in his hands. Warn cellar light off.*)

ANNE. Please, please, Mr. Van Daan. Get Father.

MR. VAN DAAN. Quiet! Quiet! (*Anne is shocked into silence. Mrs. Frank pulls her closer, holding her protectively in her arms.*)

MRS. FRANK. (*Softly, praying.*) "I lift up mine eyes unto the mountains, from whence cometh my help. My help cometh from the Lord who made heaven and earth. (*Cellar light off.*) He will not suffer thy foot to be moved. . . . He that keepeth thee will not slumber . . ." (*She stops as she hears someone coming. They all watch the door tensely. Mr. Van Daan moves to below stairwell as he sees Mr. Frank coming. Anne rushes to her father, holding him tight. Mrs. Frank and Margot rise.*)

MR. FRANK. It was a thief. That noise must have scared him away. (*Mr. Van Daan crosses below Mrs. Frank and Margot, then goes* U. C. *He begins pacing back and forth across the room.*)

MRS. VAN DAAN. Thank God.

MR. FRANK. He took the cash box. And the radio. He ran away in such a hurry that he didn't stop to shut the street door. It was swinging wide open. (*A breath of relief sweeps over them.*) I think it'd be good to have some light.

MARGOT. Are you sure it's all right? (*Site* L29. *Mantel—Margot.*)

MR. FRANK. The danger has passed. (*Margot goes to light the mantel lamp.*) Don't be so terrified, Anne. We're safe.

MR. DUSSEL. (*Crossing toward Mr. Frank to* D. C., *speaking sharply, tensely.*) Who says the danger has passed? Don't you realize we are in greater danger than ever?

MR. FRANK. Mr. Dussel, will you be still! (*Mr. Frank takes Anne back to the table, puts her in Margot's chair. He sits in his chair, trying to calm her.*)

MR. DUSSEL. (*Pointing to Peter.*) Thanks to this clumsy fool, there's someone now who knows we're up here! Someone now knows we're up here, hiding!

MRS. VAN DAAN. (*Crossing below table to Mr. Dussel.*) Someone knows we're here, yes. But who is the someone? A thief! A thief! You think a thief is going to go to the Green Police and say . . . I was robbing a place the other night and I heard a noise up over my head? You think a thief is going to do that? (*Warn house lights. House curtain.*)

MR. DUSSEL. Yes. I think he will.

MRS. VAN DAAN. (*Hysterically.*) You're crazy! (*She stumbles back to her seat at the table. Peter follows protectively, pushing Mr. Dussel aside. He sits on his stool comforting his mother. Warn* L30. *Candles out.*)

MR. DUSSEL. (*Continuing on to Mrs. Van Daan.*) I think some day he'll be caught and then he'll make a bargain with the Green Police . . . if they'll let him off, he'll tell them where some Jews are hiding! (*He goes into Right room and sinks down on his bed.*)

MR. VAN DAAN. He's right! (*From* L. C. *Mrs. Frank starts back to her place at the table.*)

ANNE. (*Terrified.*) Father, let's get out of here! We can't stay here now. . . . Let's go. . . .

62

MR. VAN DAAN. Go! Where?

MRS. FRANK. (*Sinking into her place at the table, in despair.*) Yes. Where?

MR. FRANK. (*He rises quickly, surveys the "family" as they slump in their places. He knows he must restore their courage. Mr. Van Daan is crossing to Anne's stool, where he sits facing R.*) Have we lost all faith? All courage? A moment ago we thought that they'd come for us. We were sure it was the end. But it wasn't the end. We're alive, safe. (*He prays.*) We thank Thee, Oh Lord our God, that in Thy infinite mercy Thou hast again seen fit to spare us. (*He blows out the candles, then turns to Anne. Site £30. Candles out.*) Come on, Anne. The song! The song! (*Anne starts falteringly to sing, as Mr. Frank urges her. Her voice is hardly audible at first.*)

ANNE. (*Singing.*)
"Oh, Hanukkah! Oh, Hanukkah!
The sweet celebration. . . ."

(*As she goes on singing, one by one the others join. But there is no unity, no rhythm at first. Margot slowly comes down to Mr. Frank's L. Mrs. Van Daan sobs as she sings. Mr. Dussel comes out of his room. Margot draws him into the group. As they sing, "Many are the reasons for good cheer," their courage and faith are beginning to return.*)

GROUP.
"Around the feast we gather
In complete jubilation.
Happiest of seasons
Now is here.
Many are the reasons for good cheer."
Together
We'll weather
Whatever tomorrow may bring."

(*Dim. Dim in rhythm to phrase accents. As they sing on with growing courage, THE LIGHTS START TO DIM.*)

"So hear us rejoicing
And merrily voicing
The Hanukkah song that we sing.
Hoy!"

(*House curtain. The LIGHTS ARE OUT. The CURTAIN FALLS slowly as they sing on.*)

"Hear us rejoicing
And merrily voicing
The Hanukkah song that we sing."
(House lights. Work light.)
CURTAIN

ACT II

SCENE 1

The house lights go out. In the darkness we hear Anne's Voice, again reading from the diary.

ANNE'S VOICE. Saturday, the first of January, nineteen forty-four. Another new year has begun and we find ourselves still in our hiding place. We have been here now for one year, five months, and twenty-five days. It seems that our life is at a standstill. (*Curtain. Dim up slowly. The curtain rises on a dark stage. A lead special fades up, vignetting Anne sitting at the R. end of the C. table, writing in her diary. After a moment the scene lights build around this area. It is late afternoon of a cold winter day. In the Center room Mrs. Frank, in sweater and fingerless gloves, takes down the laundry hung on a line upstage that parallels the room-dividing curtains. She exits with it above the kitchen area. Mr. Frank, also in a sweater, sits reading in his armchair at the extreme down L. corner of the room. His back is three-quarters to the audience. Margot lies on the couch with a blanket over her and the many-colored knitted scarf around her throat. Peter sits under the skylight in his room reading. He is wearing his suit jacket with the collar turned up and a knitted cap. The Van Daans are in their room. She is wearing Peter's raincoat. Mr. Van Daan is in sweater and gloves. Mr. Dussel lies asleep on his bed in the Right room. Slight changes are evident in the rooms. A faded floral print covers the lower half of the W. C. window in Anne's room. A stained antimacassar covers the back of the sofa in the Center room. Stage L. Whistles softly at rise. [Sound Cue 24.] As the LIGHTS DIM ON, Anne's Voice continues, without a break.*) We are all a little thinner. The Van Daans' "discussions" are as violent as ever. Mother still does not understand me. But then I don't understand her either. There is one great change, however. A change in myself. I read somewhere that girls of my age don't feel quite certain of

65

themselves. That they become quiet within and begin to think of the miracle that is taking place in their bodies. I think that what is happening to me is so wonderful . . . not only what can be seen, but what is taking place inside. Each time it has happened I have a feeling that I have a . . . (*Anne's voice hesitates a second. Anne looks up thinking of the proper phrase. She finds it and continues writing.*) sweet secret. (*We hear the carillon chimes begin a hymn.* [*Sound Cue 25.*] *Anne's voice fades slowly. Pause. Buzzer.*) . . . And in spite of my pain, I long for the time when I shall feel that secret within me again. (*Anne's voice is out. A pause is broken by Miep's signal on the door buzzer. Everyone is momentarily startled. Mrs. Frank hurries anxiously back into the room* U. C.)

MR. FRANK. (*Reassuring, for Mrs. Frank's benefit.*) It's Miep! (*He quickly goes down the stairs to unbolt the door. Mrs. Frank calls upstairs to the Van Daans, then crosses to knock on Peter's door on her way to the stairwell.*)

MRS. FRANK. Wake up, everyone! Miep is here! (*Sneak out lag special when Anne rises. Anne quickly finishes writing, puts diary under her arm and crosses to below the* C. *table. Margot sits up pulling the blankets around her. Mr. Dussel sits on the edge of his bed listening, disgruntled. Miep comes in with a small bunch of flowers and a bag of food. Mr. Kraler follows with a small package and more flowers. They are both bundled up against the cold.*) Miep . . . and Mr. Kraler . . . what a delightful surprise! (*After giving a warm greeting and the bag of food to Mrs. Frank, Miep crosses below her to Anne. They embrace affectionately.*)

MR. KRALER. (*Giving Mrs. Frank the package.*) We came to bring you New Year's greetings.

MRS. FRANK. You shouldn't . . . you should have at least one day to yourselves. (*She crosses above, placing the package on mantel. Mr. Kraler moves* U. L. *to greet Peter, who has come from his room.*)

ANNE. Don't say that, it's so wonderful to see them. (*Sniffing at Miep's coat.*) I can smell the wind and the cold on your clothes.

MIEP. (*Giving Anne the flowers.*) There you are. (*Then to Margot, feeling her forehead.*) How are you, Margot? . . . Feeling any better?

MARGOT. I'm all right.

ANNE. We filled her full of every kind of pill so she won't cough and make a noise. (*She runs to her room, puts diary into window-*

66

seat, and takes a glass of water from the chest, to hold her flowers. She puts them on the dressing table, then comes back to the Center room and sits R. of the C. table. The Van Daans come from upstairs. Outside there is the sound of a band playing.) [Sound Cue 26.]

MRS. VAN DAAN. Well, hello, Miep. Mr. Kraler.

MR. KRALER. (*Crossing to Mrs. Van Daan U. C., giving her the flowers.*) With my hope for peace in the New Year. (*Peter has edged to R. above the table waiting for a chance to speak to Miep.*)

PETER. (*Crossing to below C. table as Miep moves to C. below, acknowledging the Van Daans' greeting.*) Miep, have you seen Mouschi? Have you seen him anywhere around?

MIEP. I'm sorry, Peter. I asked everyone in the neighborhood had they seen a grey cat. But they said no. (*Peter retraces his steps to L. Mrs. Van Daan places her flowers in the sink. Mr. Frank comes up the stairs with two books and a small cake on a plate.*)

MR. FRANK. Look what Miep's brought for us! (*He places the cake on the C. table.*)

MRS. FRANK. (*Above table.*) A cake!

MR. VAN DAAN. A cake! (*He circles below R. end of table to Miep, pinches her cheeks gaily and continues around to the shelves.*) I'll get some plates. (*Mr. Dussel, in his room, hastily puts a coat on and starts out to join the others. Mr. Frank crosses above, placing books on mantel, then comes to U. C. to talk to Mr. Kraler. Miep moves L. to head of stairwell.*)

MRS. FRANK. Thank you, Miepia. You shouldn't have done it. You must have used all of your sugar ration for weeks. (*Giving the cake to Mrs. Van Daan, who has come down to her R.*) It's beautiful, isn't it?

MRS. VAN DAAN. (*To Miep.*) It's been ages since I even saw a cake. Not since you brought us one last year. (*She moves to below the R. end of the table. Mrs. Frank goes to stove, pours hot water into teapot, then brings it to the table.*) Remember? Don't you remember, you gave us one on New Year's Day? Just this time last year? I'll never forget it because you had "Peace in nineteen-forty-three" on it. (*She looks at the cake for the first time and reads.*) "Peace in nineteen-forty-four"!

MIEP. Well, it has to come sometime, you know. (*As Mr. Dussel comes in.*) Hello, Mr. Dussel. (*She goes quickly to U. C. to shake* his hand, then returns to D. L. *Mrs. Frank brings four cups from the drain board to the table.*)

MR. KRALER. (*To Mr. Dussel.*) How are you? (*Steps down. Shakes Mr. Dussel's hand.*)

MR. VAN DAAN. (*Brings plates, forks and a knife to the table, to Mrs. Van Daan.*) Here's the knife, liefje. Now, how many of us are there?

MIEP. None for me, thank you.

MR. KRALER. (*At the same time.*) No, thanks.

MR. FRANK. Oh, please. You must.

MIEP. I couldn't.

MR. VAN DAAN. Good! (*Mrs. Frank gets four more cups. Mrs. Van Daan continues L. and sits L. of table, placing cake on it.*) That leaves one . . . two . . . three . . . seven of us.

MR. DUSSEL. (*Steps down to R. end of table, pointing to himself.*) Eight! Eight! It's the same number as it always is!

MR. VAN DAAN. I left Margot out. I take it for granted Margot won't eat any.

ANNE. Why wouldn't she?

MRS. FRANK. (*Pouring tea.*) I think it won't harm her.

MR. VAN DAAN. All right! All right! I just didn't want her to start coughing again, that's all.

MR. DUSSEL. And please, Mrs. Frank should cut the cake. (*The Van Daans speak together.*)

MR. VAN DAAN. What's the difference?	MRS. VAN DAAN. It's not Mrs. Frank's cake, is it, Miep? It's for all of us.

MR. DUSSEL. Mrs. Frank divides things better. (*Again Mr. and Mrs. Van Daan speak at the same time.*)

MRS. VAN DAAN. (*Going to Mr. Dussel.*) What are you trying to say?	MR. VAN DAAN. Oh, come on. Stop wasting time.

MRS. VAN DAAN. (*Strides across to Mr. Dussel, who retreats two steps up and R. She confronts him. Mrs. Frank returns pot to sink.*) Don't I always give everybody exactly the same? Don't I?

MR. VAN DAAN. Forget it, Kerli. } (*Together.*)
MRS. VAN DAAN. No. I want an answer. Don't I? }

MR. DUSSEL. Yes. Yes. Everybody gets exactly the same. (*The Van Daans turn away to the cake, satisfied.*) . . . except Mr. Van

Daan always gets a little bit more. (*They whirl and come back at him, Van Daan holding the knife. Mr. Dussel retreats before their onslaught to the W. C. steps. Mrs. Frank returns to table, hands cup of tea to Miep.*)

MR. VAN DAAN. That's a lie! She always cuts the same.

MR. FRANK. Please, please! (*Apologizing as he comes down to Miep.*) You see what a little sugar cake does to us? It goes right to our heads.

MR. VAN DAAN. (*Handing Mrs. Frank the knife.*) Here you are, Mrs. Frank.

MRS. FRANK. Thank you. (*Then to Miep, as Mr. Frank comes below table to help her.*) Are you sure you won't have some?

MIEP. (*Drinking her tea.*) No, really, I have to go in a minute. (*Band fades to Center.*)

PETER. (*Coming down to Miep.*) Maybe Mouschi went back to our house . . . they say that cats . . . Do you ever get over there . . . ? I mean . . . do you suppose you could . . . ? (*The Van Daans come to L. of Mrs. Frank and he snatches the first piece. Mrs. Van Daan gets the second piece on a plate and takes it to the stove, where she stands and eats.*)

MIEP. I'll try, Peter. The first minute I get I'll try. But I'm afraid, with him gone a week . . .

MR. DUSSEL. Make up your mind, already someone has had a nice big dinner from that cat! (*Peter is furious, inarticulate. He starts toward Mr. Dussel as if to hit him. Mr. Frank stops him. Mrs. Frank speaks quickly to ease the situation.*)

MRS. FRANK. (*To Miep, as she hands cake to Mr. Dussel.*) This is delicious, Miep!

MRS. VAN DAAN. (*Eating hers.*) Delicious!

MR. VAN DAAN. (*Sitting in chair above stairwell, wolfing his cake. Peter moves to U. L. Mr. Frank is R. of Mrs. Frank. Mrs. Frank gives cake to him and Anne.*) Dirk's in luck to get a girl who can bake like this!

MIEP. (*Putting down her empty tea cup on the table.*) I have to run. Dirk's taking me to a party tonight. (*Mrs. Frank takes cake to Margot, then puts remaining pieces on plates.*)

ANNE. (*To Miep.*) How heavenly! Remember now what every-one is wearing, and what you have to eat and everything, so you can tell us tomorrow.

MIEP. I'll give you a full report! Good-bye, everyone. (*She starts downstairs.*)

MR. VAN DAAN. (*To Miep.*) Just a minute. There's something I'd like you to do for me. (*Mr. Van Daan hurries off up the stairs to the Attic room. Mrs. Van Daan looks after him fearfully.*)

MRS. VAN DAAN. (*Sharply.*) Putti, where are you going? (*She starts after him, calling hysterically.*) What do you want? Putti, what are you going to do? (*She rushes up the stairs after him.*)

MIEP. (*To Peter.*) What's wrong?

PETER. (*His sympathy is with his mother.*) Father says he's going to sell her fur coat. She's crazy about that old fur coat.

MR. DUSSEL. Is it possible? Is it possible that anyone is so silly as to worry about a fur coat in times like this?

PETER. (*Advances on Mr. Dussel, but is stopped by Mr. Frank. Mrs. Frank sits above c. table on padded stool.*) It's none of your darn business . . . and if you say one more thing . . . I'll—I'll take you and I'll . . . I mean it . . . I'll . . . (*Suddenly there is a piercing scream from Mrs. Van Daan above. She grabs at the fur coat as Mr. Van Daan passes her to go downstairs with it.*)

MRS. VAN DAAN. No! No! No! Don't you dare take that! You hear? It's mine! (*Peter, embarrassed, miserable, goes to stairs but can do nothing.*) My father gave me that! You didn't give it to me. You have no right. Let go of it . . . you hear? (*Mr. Van Daan pulls the coat from her hands and hurries downstage. Mrs. Van Daan sinks on the floor, sobbing. Mr. Van Daan hurries down the stairs. As he comes into the Center room, the people look away, embarrassed for him.*)

MR. VAN DAAN. (*To Mr. Kraler, from u. c.*) Just a little— discussion over the advisability of selling this coat. As I have often reminded Mrs. Van Daan, it's very selfish of her to keep it when people outside are in such desperate need of clothing. . . . (*He gives the coat to Miep.*) So if you will please to sell it for us? It should fetch a good price. (*An afterthought as Miep turns to go.*) And by the way, will you get me cigarettes? I don't care what kind they are . . . get all you can.

MIEP. It's terribly difficult to get them, Mr. Van Daan. But I'll try. Good-bye.

MRS. FRANK. Good-bye.

MR. FRANK. Good-bye, Miep. (*She goes. Mr. Frank follows her*

70

down the steps to bolt the door after her. Mrs. Frank gives Mr. Kraler a cup of tea.)

MRS. FRANK. Are you sure you won't have some cake, Mr. Kraler?

MR. KRALER. *(A step toward Mrs. Frank.)* I'd better not. *(Fade band to R.)*

MR. VAN DAAN. *(Coming to Mr. Kraler's L.)* You're still feeling badly? What does the doctor say?

MR. KRALER. I haven't been to him.

MRS. FRANK. Now, Mr. Kraler! . . .

MR. KRALER. *(Takes cup with him as he moves down, sitting L. of table.)* Oh, I tried. But you can't get near a doctor these days . . . they're so busy. After weeks I finally managed to get one on the telephone. I told him I'd like an appointment. . . . I wasn't feeling very well. You know what he answers . . . over the telephone . . . Stick out your tongue! *(They laugh. He turns to Mr. Frank as Mr. Frank comes back, and sits in chair D. L. Mr. Van Daan gets tea and moves to mantel. Mrs. Frank gives tea to Mr. Dussel, cake and tea to Peter, who sits on W. C. steps to eat.)* I have some contracts here. . . . I wonder if you'd look over them with me. . . .

MR. FRANK. *(Putting out his hand for them.)* Of course.

MR. KRALER. *(He rises.)* If we could go downstairs . . . *(Mr. Frank starts ahead, Mr. Kraler speaks to the others.)* Will you forgive us? I won't keep him but a minute. *(He starts to follow Mr. Frank down the stairs.)*

MARGOT. *(With sudden foreboding.)* What's happened? Something's happened! Hasn't it, Mr. Kraler? *(Mr. Kraler stops and comes back to C. below table, trying to reassure Margot with a pretense of casualness.)*

MR. KRALER. No, really. I want your father's advice . . .

MARGOT. Something's gone wrong! I know it!

MR. FRANK. *(Coming back, to Mr. Kraler.)* If it's something that concerns us here, it's better that we all hear it.

MR. KRALER. *(Turning to him, quietly.)* But . . . the children . . . ?

MR. FRANK. What they'd imagine would be worse than any reality. *(Mr. Frank sits D. L. Mr. Kraler is reluctant, but begins his story. They all listen with intense apprehension and move slowly to sit: Mrs. Frank above the table, Mr. Van Daan on the*

*upstage end of the sofa. Mr. Dussel puts cup and plate on mantel,
then steps toward* C., *Peter rises and moves in.*)

MR. KRALER. It's a man in the storeroom. . . . (*As he speaks
to Mr. Frank, he circles* L. *to above chair* L. *of table.*) I don't
know whether or not you remember him . . . Carl, about fifty,
heavy-set, near-sighted. . . . He came with us just before you
left. (*Band fades out.*)

MR. FRANK. He was from Utrecht?

MR. KRALER. That's the man. A couple of weeks ago, when I was
in the storeroom, he closed the door and asked me . . . How's
Mr. Frank? What do you hear from Mr. Frank? I told him I only
knew there was a rumor that you were in Switzerland. He said
he'd heard that rumor too, but he thought I might know something
more. I didn't pay any attention to it . . . but then a thing happened yesterday. . . . He'd brought some invoices to the office
for me to sign. As I was going through them, I looked up. He was
standing staring at the bookcase . . . the bookcase that hides your
door. (*Indicating the door at the foot of the stairwell.*) He said he
thought he remembered a door there . . . wasn't there a door
there that used to go up to the loft? Then he told me he wanted
more money. Twenty guilders more a week. (*Sits* L. *of table. Mrs.
Van Daan comes slowly downstairs and sits on bottom step, listening.*)

MR. VAN DAAN. (*Bursting out.*) Blackmail!

MR. FRANK. (*Calmly.*) Twenty guilders? Very modest blackmail.

MR. VAN DAAN. That's just the beginning.

MR. DUSSEL. (*Nervously rushing down* L. *of table to Mr.
Frank.*) You know what I think? He was the thief who was down
there that night. That's how he knows we're here.

MR. FRANK. (*To Mr. Kraler, as Mr. Dussel returns to* U. R. C.)
How was it left? What did you tell him?

MR. KRALER. I said I had to think about it. What shall I do?
Pay him the money? . . . Take a chance on firing him . . . or
what? I don't know.

MR. DUSSEL. (*Warn phone. More agitated as he returns to Mr.
Frank.*) For God's sake don't fire him. Pay him what he asks . . .
keep him here where you can have your eye on him.

MR. FRANK. (*To Mr. Kraler.*) Is it so much that he's asking?
What are they paying nowadays? (*Mr. Dussel moves* U. C. *again.*)

MR. KRALER. He could get it in a war plant. But this isn't a war plant. (*Turns to reassure the others.*) Mind you, I don't know if he really knows . . . or if he doesn't know.

MR. FRANK. Offer him half. Then we'll soon find out if it's blackmail or not.

MR. DUSSEL. (*Running to Mr. Frank again.*) And if it is? We've got to pay it, haven't we? Anything he asks we've got to pay.

MR. FRANK. (*Patiently, calmly.*) Let's decide that when the time comes.

MR. KRALER. (*Again trying to reassure them. Mr. Dussel moves* u. l.) This may be all my imagination. You get to a point, these days, where you suspect everyone and everything. Again and again . . . on some simple look or word, I've found myself . . . (*Phone. The telephone rings in the office below.*)

MRS. VAN DAAN. (*Hurrying to* l. *of Mr. Kraler, breathless, overwrought.*) There's the telephone! What does that mean, the telephone ringing on a holiday?

MR. KRALER. That's my wife. I told her I had to go over some papers in my office . . . to call me there when she got out of church. (*Rises.*) I'll offer him half then. (*Shakes Mr. Frank's hand.*) Good-bye . . . we'll hope for the best! (*Phone stops. Site. The group call their good-byes half-heartedly. Mr. Frank follows Mr. Kraler to bolt the door below. Mrs. Frank rises to see Mr. Kraler out and then sits dispirited in the chair above the stairwell. After a moment Mr. Van Daan slaps his knee in a gesture of resignation, then takes his and Margot's china to the sink. Mrs. Van Daan crosses above and enters the* W. C. *Peter puts his cup and plate on sink, then sits* c. *above table.*)

MR. DUSSEL. (*To Mr. Van Daan.*) You can thank your son for this . . . (*Pointing to the hanging lamp.*) smashing the light! I tell you, it's just a question of time now. (*He goes up, standing looking out the window* u. c. *Warn L40A. W. C. on.*)

MARGOT. Sometimes I wish the end would come . . . whatever it is.

MRS. FRANK. (*Rises, shocked.*) Margot! (*Anne goes to Margot, sitting beside her on the couch with her arms around her.*)

MARGOT. Then at least we'd know where we were.

MRS. FRANK. (*Crossing below to* R. C.) You should be ashamed of yourself! Talking that way! Think how lucky we are! Think of the thousands dying in the war, every day! Think of the people in concentration camps! (*W. C. on.*)

ANNE. (*Lashing out at her mother.*) What's the good of that? What's the good of thinking of misery when you're already miserable? That's stupid!

MRS. FRANK. (*Shocked.*) Anne! (*As Anne goes on, Mr. Frank comes back up the steps, and listens unhappily.*)

ANNE. We're young, Margot and Peter and I! (*Rising.*) You grownups have had your chance! But look at us. . . . If we begin thinking of all the horror in the world, we're lost! We're trying to hold on to some kind of ideals . . . when everything . . . ideals, hopes . . . everything, are being destroyed!

MRS. FRANK. (*She moves up to* L. *of Anne, trying to get in a word.*) Now, Anne . . .

ANNE. (*Overriding her.*) It isn't our fault that the world is in such a mess! We weren't around when all this started!

MRS. FRANK. Anne!

ANNE. So don't try to take it out on us! (*Anne rushes off to her room, slamming the door after her. She picks up a brush from the chest and hurls it to the floor. Then she sits on her bed, trying to control her anger.*)

MR. VAN DAAN. (*Coming to above table,* R. *of Peter.*) She talks as if we started the war! Did we start the war? (*Mr. Van Daan sees Anne's cake on the table. He reaches out to take it, but Peter anticipates him, picking up the plate.*)

PETER. She left her cake. (*Peter crosses toward Anne's door. Mr. Van Daan looks after him, turns up to the sink, puts down his cup, and goes upstairs, disappearing* R. *Mr. Frank gives Mrs. Frank her cake. She sits above table facing* L., *eating without relish. He then takes a piece to Margot and sits quietly on the sofa above her as she eats slowly. Peter has entered the doorway of Anne's darkened room. She sits up quickly, trying to hide the signs of her tears. With the cake.*) You left this.

ANNE. (*Dully.*) Thanks. (*He places cake on window seat, then moves back to door. He changes his mind, closes the door and turns to her. As he speaks he works back to the window seat Warn L 41. Anne's bracket on, Mr. Dussel.*)

PETER. I thought you were fine just now. You know just how to talk to them. You know just how to say it. I'm no good. . . . I never can think . . . especially when I'm mad. . . . That Dussel . . . when he said that about Mouschi! . . . someone eating him . . . all I could think is . . . I wanted to hit him. I wanted to give him such a . . . a . . . that he'd . . . that's what I used to do when there was an argument at school . . . that's the way I . . . but here . . . and an old man like that . . . it wouldn't be so good.

ANNE. You're making a big mistake about me. I do it all wrong. I say too much. I go too far. I hurt people's feelings. . . . (*Mr. Dussel leaves the window up* C., *starting for the Right room.*)

PETER. I think you're just fine . . . what I want to say . . . if it wasn't for you around here, I don't know. What I mean . . . (*Site L 41. Peter is interrupted by Mr. Dussel's turning on the lights. [Wall bracket.] The two young people turn to look at him. Mr. Dussel pauses a second staring back, then moves toward his bed. Peter advances toward him, slowly, menacingly. Mr. Dussel retreats, backing out the door. He looks back forlornly, as Peter firmly shuts the door on him.*)

ANNE. (*As Peter returns.*) Do you mean it, Peter? Do you really mean it?

PETER. I said it, didn't I?

ANNE. Thank you, Peter! (*During the following scene, Mr. Dussel, lost, wanders across* L. *to the door of Peter's room. After a moment's hesitation, he enters, and sits under the skylight to read one of Peter's books.*)

PETER. (*Looking at the pictures on the wall.*) You've got quite a collection.

ANNE. (*She rises.*) Wouldn't you like some in your room? I could give you some. (*Sitting on dressing table stool.*) Heaven knows you spend enough time in there . . . doing Heaven knows what. . . .

PETER. (R. *of her.*) It's easier. A fight starts, or an argument . . . I duck in there.

ANNE. You're lucky, having a room to go to. (*It is at this point that Mr. Dussel enters Peter's room.*) His lordship is always here. . . . I hardly ever get a minute alone. When they start in on me, I can't duck away. I have to stand there and take it.

PETER. You gave some of it back just now. (*Margot cannot finish the cake. She gives it to Mr. Frank, who places it on the lamp table, then helps her lie comfortably again and tucks her in. Mrs. Frank stacks china and silver on table, then takes it to the sink. Mr. Frank collects all she cannot manage and takes it to her. She washes as he dries.*)

75

ANNE. (*During this.*) I get so mad. They've formed their opinions . . . about everything . . . but we . . . we're still trying to find out. . . . We have problems here that no other people our age have ever had. And just as you think you've solved them, something comes along and bang! You have to start all over again.

PETER. At least you've got someone you can talk to. (*Warn change. Curtain light on.*)

ANNE. Not really. Mother . . . I never discuss anything serious with her. She doesn't understand. Father's all right. We can talk about everything . . . everything but one thing. Mother. He simply won't talk about her. I don't think you can be reall·· intimate with anyone if he holds something back, do you?

PETER. I think your father's fine.

ANNE. Oh, he is, Peter! He is! He's the only one who's ever given me the feeling that I have any sense. But anyway, nothing can take the place of school and friends of your own age . . . or near your age . . . can it?

PETER. I suppose you miss your friends and all.

ANNE. It isn't just . . . (*She breaks off, staring up at him a second.*) Isn't it funny, you and I? Here we've been seeing each other every minute for almost a year and a half, and this is the first time we've ever really talked. It helps a lot to have someone to talk to, don't you think? It helps you to let off steam.

PETER. (*Edging to the door.*) Well, any time you want to let off steam, you can come into my room.

ANNE. (*Following him.*) I can get up an awful lot of steam. You'll have to be careful how you say that.

PETER. It's all right with me.

ANNE. Do you mean it?

PETER. I said it, didn't I? (*He goes out. Anne stands in her doorway looking after him. As he gets to his door he stands for a moment, looking back at her. Then he goes in, shutting the door. Mr. Dussel rises as Peter comes in, and quickly passes him, going out. Anne sees Mr. Dussel as he comes into the Center room, and pulls her door shut. Mr. Dussel turns back toward Peter's room. Peter pulls his door shut. Mr. Dussel stands there, bewildered, forlorn. On second slam dim med. fast 1-2-3-4. Drop in. Work light on. Curtain light on. The scene lights fade smoothly, leaving Mr. Dussel in a lag special which fades quickly. The black drop is brought in. Anne's voice is heard in the darkness, faintly at first, then with growing strength.)*

ANNE'S VOICE. We've had bad news. The people from whom Miep got our ration books have been arrested. So we have had to cut down on our food. Our stomachs are so empty that they rumble and make strange noises, all in different keys. Mr. Van Daan's is deep and low, like a bass fiddle. Mine is high, whistling like a flute. As we all sit around waiting for supper, it's like an orchestra tuning up. It only needs Toscanini to raise his baton and we'd be off in the Ride of the Valkyries. Monday, the sixth of March, nineteen-forty-four. Mr. Kraler is in the hospital. It seems he has ulcers. Pim says we are his ulcers. Miep has to run the business and us too. The Americans have landed on the southern tip of Italy. Father looks for a quick finish to the war. Mr. Dussel is waiting every day for the warehouse man to demand more money. Have I been skipping too much from one subject to another? I can't help it. *(W. L. off. Drop out. Black drop out.)* I feel that Spring is coming. *(Lights begin slowly dimming up. Voice starts to fade.)* I feel it in my whole body and soul. I feel utterly confused. I am longing . . . so longing . . . for everything . . . for friends . . . *(Voice out. Lights three-quarters full and rising.)* for someone to talk to . . . someone who understands . . . someone young, who feels as I do. . . . *(Dim up slow.)*

ACT II

Scene 2

It is evening, after supper. From outside we hear the sound of children playing and whistles in the distance. (Sound Cue 27.) The grownups, with the exception of Mr. Van Daan, are all in the Center room. He is sitting in his bedroom working on a piece of embroidery in an embroidery frame. Mrs. Frank is in the chair D. L. mending a glove. Mrs. Van Daan sits R. of the C. table, reading a fashion magazine. Mr. Frank is below the table, sitting on the padded stool, going over some business ledgers. Mr. Dussel shifts impatiently from foot to foot outside the door of

77

his room. All lamps are lighted. In his bedroom Peter sits on the foot of his bed combing his hair before a small mirror set up on the window seat. As the scene goes on he puts on his tie, buffs his shoes, brushes his coat and puts it on, and makes certain his room is neat. He is preparing for a visit from Anne. The blackout curtain covers the skylight. His lamp is on. A group of photographs is now on the L. wall. One is tilted a bit. On the other side of the stage Anne, too, is getting dressed. She stands in her slip before the mirror on her dressing table, putting up her hair. Margot is seated on Anne's bed, stitching the waistband of a skirt for Anne to wear. The sewing basket is beside her. Both lights are on. When the lights are full, Mr. Dussel crosses impatiently L. above. He stops to glance back at the door, then strides down to Mrs. Frank, looking at her, appealing for help. She becomes more absorbed in her sewing. He stamps across to the couch. Mrs. Frank looks after him unhappily. Mr. Dussel sits on the couch, pops up immediately, and goes to the door of the Right room. He raps sharply.

ANNE. (*Calling to him.*) No, no, Mr. Dussel! I am not dressed yet. (*Mr. Dussel walks away, furious, sitting on the couch and burying his head in his hands. Anne turns to Margot.*) How is that? How does that look?

MARGOT. (*Glancing at her briefly.*) Fine.

ANNE. You didn't even look.

MARGOT. Of course I did. It's fine.

ANNE. Margot, tell me, am I terribly ugly? (*Mrs. Frank, in the Center room, feeling sorry for Mr. Dussel, crosses above toward Anne's door. Mr. Dussel half rises and Mrs. Frank motions him to be patient. He sits.*)

MARGOT. (*To Anne.*) Oh, stop fishing.

ANNE. No. No. Tell me.

MARGOT. Of course you're not. You've got nice eyes . . . and a lot of animation, and . . .

ANNE. (*Drily.*) A little vague, aren't you? (*She reaches over and takes a brassiere of Margot's out of the sewing basket. She tries it on over her slip.*)

MRS. FRANK. (*Knocking.*) May I come in?

78

MARGOT. Come in, Mother.

MRS. FRANK. (*Coming in and closing the door behind her.*) Mr. Dussel's impatient to get in here.

ANNE. Heavens, he takes the room for himself the entire day.

MRS. FRANK. (*Gently.*) Anne, dear, you're not going in again tonight to see Peter?

ANNE. (*With dignity.*) That is my intention. (*She crosses to the mirror to study effect of the brassiere.*)

MRS. FRANK. But you've already spent a great deal of time in there today.

ANNE. I was in there exactly twice. Once to get the dictionary, and then three-quarters of an hour before supper. (*She turns to view herself from another angle.*)

MRS. FRANK. Aren't you afraid you're disturbing him?

ANNE. Mother, I have some intuition.

MRS. FRANK. Then may I ask you this much, Anne. Please don't shut the door when you go in.

ANNE. You sound like Mrs. Van Daan! (*She throws the brassiere back in Margot's sewing basket and picks up her blouse, putting it on as she returns to the dressing table.*)

MRS. FRANK. No. No. I don't mean to suggest anything wrong. I only wish that you wouldn't expose yourself to criticism . . . that you wouldn't give Mrs. Van Daan the opportunity to be unpleasant.

ANNE. Mrs. Van Daan doesn't need an opportunity to be unpleasant!

MRS. FRANK. Everyone's on edge, worried about Mr. Kraler. This is one more thing . . .

ANNE. I'm sorry, Mother. I'm going to Peter's room. I'm not going to let Petronella Van Daan spoil our friendship. (*Mrs. Frank hesitates for a second, then goes out, closing the door after her. Mr. Dussel looks up and she indicates it won't be long now. She continues to shelves, gets pack of cards, puts down gloves, and sits L. of table playing solitaire. When Mrs. Frank leaves, Anne comes down to Margot, indicating she would like to wear her high heels. Margot smiles agreement and Anne hands her a piece of paper from their dressing table for Margot to put into the shoes. Margot gives skirt to Anne and slips off her shoes. As she speaks she stuffs the paper into the shoes.*)

MARGOT (*To Anne.*) Why don't you two talk in the main

room? It'd save a lot of trouble. It's hard on Mother, having to listen to those remarks from Mrs. Van Daan and not say a word.

ANNE. (*Getting into skirt.*) Why doesn't she say a word? I think it's ridiculous to take it and take it.

MARGOT. You don't understand Mother at all, do you? She can't talk back. She's not like you. It's just not in her nature to fight back.

ANNE. Anyway . . . the only one I worry about is you. I feel awfully guilty about you. (*She sits on the stool, putting on Margot's high-heeled shoes.*)

MARGOT. What about?

ANNE. I mean, every time I go into Peter's room, I have a feeling I may be hurting you. (*Margot shakes her head. Anne sits on foot of bed with Margot.*) I know if it were me, I'd be wild. I'd be desperately jealous, if it were me.

MARGOT. Well, I'm not.

ANNE. You don't feel badly? Really? Truly? You're not jealous?

MARGOT. Of course I'm jealous . . . jealous that you've got something to get up in the morning for. . . . But jealous of you and Peter? No.

ANNE. (*As she returns to the mirror.*) Maybe there's nothing to be jealous of. Maybe he doesn't really like me. Maybe I'm just taking the place of his cat! (*She picks up a pair of short white gloves, putting them on.*) Wouldn't you like to come in with us? (*On laugh warn L 43 A. Anne's bracket off—Margot.*)

MARGOT. I have a book. (*In the Center room Mr. Dussel can stand it no longer. He jumps up, going to the bedroom door and knocks sharply.*)

MR. DUSSEL. Will you please let me in my room!

ANNE. Just a minute, dear, dear Mr. Dussel. (*She picks up her mother's pink stole and adjusts it elegantly over her shoulders, then gives a last look in the mirror. She goes to door, then turns to speak to Margot, who has come up R. of her.*) Well, here I go . . . to run the gauntlet. (*She comes out, followed by Margot, who turns off the wall bracket. Site L 43 A. Anne's bracket-off—Margot.*)

MR. DUSSEL. (*Sarcastic.*) Thank you so much. (*Anne gives him a dignified bow. He goes into his room and closes the door. Anne starts to cross below the table, trying to appear very sophisticated.*)

MRS. VAN DAAN. My God, look at her! (*Anne pays no atten-*

tion and continues toward Peter's room. Margot's heels give her a bit of trouble, but her head is high. Mr. Dussel, in Right room, gets trousers from hook D. R., *scissors from chest and sits on his bed trimming frayed cuffs. Margot takes her sewing basket to the shelves* U. L., *gets her crossword puzzle book and pencil. Anne knocks at Peter's door. He makes a quick check to see all is in order.)* I don't know what good it is to have a son. I never see him. He wouldn't care if I killed myself. *(Peter opens the door and stands aside for Anne to come in.)* Just a minute, Anne! *(She crosses above to them at the door. Margot brings book to sofa, adjusts lamp and sits working a puzzle.)* I'd like to say a few words to my son. Do you mind? *(Peter and Anne stand waiting.)* Peter, I don't want you staying up till all hours tonight. You've got to have your sleep. You're a growing boy. You hear?

MRS. FRANK. Anne won't stay late. She's going to bed promptly at nine. Aren't you, Anne?

ANNE. Yes, Mother. *(Too sweetly to Mrs. Van Daan.)* May we go now? *(Sound of children playing fades to* R.)

MRS. VAN DAAN. Are you asking me? I didn't know I had anything to say about it.

MRS. FRANK. Listen for the chimes, Anne dear. *(The two young people go off into Peter's room, shutting the door after them.)*

MRS. VAN DAAN. *(Dropping to* L. *of Mrs. Frank.)* In my day it was the boys who called on the girls.

MRS. FRANK. You know how young people like to feel that they have secrets. Peter's room is the only place where they can talk.

MRS. VAN DAAN. Talk! That's not what they called it when I was young. *(L43B. General dim* C. *room. Mrs. Van Daan crosses above, puts her magazine on the mantel, goes to the sink, picks up her apron and starts to polish the coffee pot. Peter comes to* L. *of Anne. She turns to him, indignant.)*

ANNE. Aren't they awful? Aren't they impossible? Treating us as if we're still in the nursery.

PETER. Don't let it bother you. It doesn't bother me.

ANNE. I suppose you can't really blame them. *(Crossing down, she sits on foot of Peter's bed facing front.)* . . . they think back to what they were like at our age. They don't realize how much more advanced we are . . . when I think what wonderful discussions we've had! *(Warn* W. C. *on.)* . . Oh, I forgot. I was going to bring you some more pictures.

PETER. (*Picking up bottle of orange soda and two glasses from his box-table.*) Oh, these are fine, thanks.

ANNE. Don't you want some more? Miep just brought me some new ones.

PETER. Maybe later. (*He comes down and sits on the window seat facing her. He hands her a glass and pours soda into it, then takes some for himself. In the Center room Mrs. Van Daan puts down the coffee pot and goes to the W. C. and turns on the light. W. C. on.*)

ANNE. (*Looking at one of the photographs.*) I remember when I got that . . . I won it. I bet Jopie that I could eat five ice cream cones. We'd all been playing ping-pong. . . . We used to have heavenly times . . . we'd finish up with ice cream at the Delphi, or the Oasis, where Jews were allowed . . . there'd always be a lot of boys . . . we'd laugh and joke. . . . I'd like to go back to it for a few days or a week. But after that I know I'd be bored to death. I think more seriously about life now. I want to be a journalist . . . or something. I love to write. What do you want to do? (*Mr. Frank takes his ledgers, moves R. Margot stops him and asks for help on a word. He can't make a suggestion and continues to the shelves, puts down the books and gets small chess set. He completes circle to below the table. He and Mrs. Frank play.*)

PETER. I thought I might go off some place . . . work on a farm or something . . . some job that doesn't take much brains.

ANNE. You shouldn't talk that way. You've got the most awful inferiority complex.

PETER. I know I'm not smart.

ANNE. That isn't true. You're much better than I am in dozens of things . . . arithmetic and algebra and . . . Well, you're a million times better than I am in algebra. (*With sudden directness.*) You like Margot, don't you? Right from the start you liked her, liked her much better than me.

PETER. (*Uncomfortably.*) Oh, I don't know. (*Mr. Dussel replaces trousers on hook, gets nail file from dressing table and sits on bed filing his nails.*)

ANNE. It's all right. Everyone feels that way. Margot's so good. She's sweet and bright and beautiful and I'm not.

PETER. I wouldn't say that.

ANNE. Oh, no, I'm not. I know that. I know quite well that I'm not a beauty. I never have been and never shall be.

PETER. I don't agree at all. I think you're pretty.

ANNE. That's not true!

PETER. And another thing. You've changed . . . from at first, I mean.

ANNE. I have?

PETER. I used to think you were awful noisy.

ANNE. (*Eagerly.*) And what do you think now, Peter? How have I changed?

PETER. Well . . . er . . . you're . . . quieter.

ANNE. (*Amused.*) I'm glad you don't just hate me.

PETER. I never said that.

ANNE. I bet when you get out of here you'll never think of me again.

PETER. That's crazy.

ANNE. When you get back with all of your friends, you're going to say . . . now what did I ever see in that Mrs. Quack Quack?

PETER. I haven't got any friends.

ANNE. Oh, Peter, of course you have. Everyone has friends.

PETER. Not me. I don't want any. I get along all right without them.

ANNE. Does that mean you can get along without me? I think of myself as your friend.

PETER. No. If they were all like you, it'd be different. (*Peter realizes what he has said. To cover his embarrassment he hurriedly picks up the glasses and bottle, returning them to the box-table. There is a second's silence and then Annie speaks, hesitantly, shyly. She cannot look at him. Warn W. C. off.*)

ANNE. Peter, did you ever kiss a girl?

PETER. Yes. Once.

ANNE. (*She looks quickly back over shoulder at him. Then to cover her feelings.*) That picture's crooked. (*Peter straightens the picture. She is looking away again.*) Was she pretty?

PETER. Huh?

ANNE. The girl that you kissed.

PETER. I don't know. I was blindfolded. (*He comes back and resumes his place opposite her.*) It was at a party. One of those kissing games. (*W. C. off. Mrs. Van Daan turns off W. C. light and comes into Center room and polishes the coffee pot at the sink.*)

83

ANNE. (*Relieved.*) Oh. I don't suppose that really counts, does it? (*Warn W. C. on.*)

PETER. It didn't with me. (*Mr. Dussel gets his pajamas and starts for the W. C.*)

ANNE. I've been kissed twice. Once a man I'd never seen before kissed me on the cheek when he picked me up off the ice and I was crying. And the other was Mr. Koophuis, a friend of Father's who kissed my hand. You wouldn't say those counted, would you?

PETER. I wouldn't say so.

ANNE. I know almost for certain that Margot would never kiss anyone unless she was engaged to them. And I'm sure too that Mother never touched a man before Pim. But I don't know . . . things (*Mr. Dussel goes into W. C. and turns on the light.*) are so different now. . . . (*W. C. on.*) What do you think? Do you think a girl shouldn't kiss anyone except if she's engaged or something? It's so hard to try to think what to do, when here we are with the whole world falling around our ears and you think . . . well . . . you don't know what's going to happen tomorrow and . . . What do you think?

PETER. I suppose it'd depend on the girl. Some girls, anything they do's wrong. But others . . . well . . . it wouldn't necessarily be wrong with them. (*The carillon starts to strike nine o'clock.*) [*Sound Cue 28.*] I've always thought that when two people . . . (*Warn L44. Warn change. Curtain light on.*)

ANNE. Nine o'clock. I have to go.

PETER. That's right.

ANNE. (*Without moving.*) Good night. (*Their faces are close together. There is a second's pause. Then Peter, too shy to kiss her, moves upstage.*)

PETER. You won't let them stop you coming?

ANNE. No. (*She rises and starts for the door, then turns back to him.*) Some time I might bring my diary. There are so many things in it that I want to talk over with you. There's a lot about you.

PETER. What kind of thing?

ANNE. I wouldn't want you to see some of it. I thought you were a nothing, just the way you thought about me.

PETER. Did you change your mind, the way I changed my mind about you?

ANNE. Well—you'll see . . . (*For a second Anne stands looking* up at Peter, longing for him to kiss her. As he makes no move she turns to go. Then suddenly he grabs her arm and turning her around, holds her awkwardly in his arms, kissing her on the cheek. Anne floats slowly out, dazed. She stands for a minute, her back to the people in the Center room, shutting the door of his room after her. After a moment her poise returns. Site [shawl biz] L44. Gen. dim—Peter's room. She flips one end of her scarf back over her shoulder. Then she goes to her father and mother at the c. table, silently kissing them good night. They murmur their good nights. She crosses to Margot, kisses her, and then continues up, and opens the door to her room. Suddenly she is aware of Mrs. Van Daan at the sink. She goes quickly up to her. She takes Mrs. Van Daan's face in her hands and kisses her first on one cheek, then on the other. Then she goes off into her room, shutting the door. Mr. and Mrs. Frank have watched Anne. They return to their game. Mrs. Van Daan comes slowly down to above the c. table, watching Anne go. Then she looks slowly across toward Peter's room. Her suspicions are confirmed.)

MRS. VAN DAAN. (She knows.) Ah hah! (Dim fast. Drop in. Work light on. Curtain light on. The scene lights fade swiftly, leaving her shaking her head knowingly in a lag special. It fades quickly. The black drop is brought in and we hear Anne's voice in the darkness, faintly at first, then with growing strength.)

ANNE'S VOICE. By this time we all know each other so well that if anyone starts to tell a story, the rest can finish it for him. We're having to cut down still further on our meals. What makes it worse, the rats have been at work again. They've carried off some of our precious food. Even Mr. Dussel wishes now that Mouschi was here. Thursday, the twentieth of April, nineteen forty-four. Invasion fever is mounting every day. Miep tells us that people outside talk of nothing else. For myself, life has become much more pleasant. I often go to Peter's room after supper. Oh, don't think I'm in love, because I'm not. But it does make life more bearable to have someone with whom you can exchange views. No more tonight. P.S. . . . I must be honest. I must confess that I actually live for the next meeting. (Work light off.) Is there anything lovelier than to sit under the skylight and feel the sun on your cheeks and have a darling boy in your arms? (Worklight out. Black drop rises.) I admit now that I'm glad (Drop out.) the Van Daans had a son (Dim up-med.) and not a daughter. (Lights *begin to fade up. Voice begins to fade out.)* I've outgrown another dress. That's the third. I'm having to wear Margot's clothes after all. I'm working hard on my French . . . *(Voice out. Lights three-quarters full and rising.)* . . . and am now reading "LaBelle Nivernaise." *(Warn L50. Hanging Lamp. On—Margot.)*

ACT II

SCENE 3

It is night, a few weeks later. Everyone is in bed. All is quiet except for faint harbor whistles in the distance. (Sound Cue 29.) A dim cool light falls through the skylight in Peter's room. The cyclorama is slightly illuminated.

We can faintly see Mr. and Mrs. Frank and Anne in their beds. Margot sleeps U. L. behind the drawn curtain. Suddenly in the Van Daans' room a match flares up for a moment and then is quickly put out. Mr. Van Daan, in bare feet, dressed in underwear and trousers, is dimly seen coming stealthily down the stairs and into the Center room. He goes to the food safe and again lights a match. Then he cautiously opens the safe, taking out a half loaf of bread. As he closes the safe, it creaks. He stands rigid. Mrs. Frank sits up in bed. She sees him.

MRS. FRANK. *(Screaming.)* Otto! Otto! Come quick! *(The rest of the people wake, hurriedly getting up.)*

MR. FRANK. What is it? What's happened? *(Mr. Van Daan starts for stairs, becomes confused and continues across to U. L. Margot hurriedly gets stool above stove and drags it under hanging lamp.)*

MRS. FRANK. *(As she rushes over to Mr. Van Daan.)* He's stealing the food!

MR. DUSSEL. *(Dashing out of his room toward Mr. Van Daan. Anne follows after throwing skirt over her shoulders like a shawl. She holds U. R.)* You! You! Give me that.

86

MRS. VAN DAAN. (*Getting out of bed. The following speeches overlap.*) Putti . . . Putti . . . what is it?

MR. DUSSEL. (*Grabbing the bread in Mr. Van Daan's hands as Mr. Van Daan backs downstage to L. Margot must be ready with hand on hanging lamp on "good-for-nothing."*) You dirty thief . . . stealing food . . . you good-for-nothing . . . (*£50. Hanging lamp on.*)

MR. FRANK. (*His arms around Mr. Dussel's waist, he tugs upstage.*) Mr. Dussel! For God's sake! Help me, Peter! (*Peter has come out of his room, squeezed downstage of his father and is pulling at his shoulders.*)

PETER. Let him go! Let go! (*When hanging lamp goes on, Mr. Dussel and Mr. Frank give a tug that pulls Mr. Van Daan to his knees. Mr. Dussel has the bread. Mr. Van Daan rises quickly and retreats below to D. R. C.*)

MR. DUSSEL. You greedy, selfish . . .

MRS. VAN DAAN. (*Coming down the stairs.*) Putti . . . what is it? (*All of Mrs. Frank's gentleness, her self-control is gone. She is outraged, in a frenzy of indignation.*)

MRS. FRANK. (u. c., *shielding eyes from sudden glare.*) The bread! He was stealing the bread!

MR. DUSSEL. (*Coming to above L. end of table where he places the bread. Peter sits, humiliated, on stairs L.*) It was you, and all the time we thought it was the rats!

MR. FRANK. (*At L.*) Mr. Van Daan, how could you!

MR. VAN DAAN. (D. R. C. *facing R.*) I'm hungry. (*Mr. Dussel crosses to his room and puts on his suit jacket. Then he crosses above and sits in the round chair L. above stairwell. Mrs. Van Daan moves protectively around R. end of table to Mr. Van Daan, stands L. of him.*)

MRS. FRANK. (*With righteous rage.*) We're all of us hungry! I see the children getting thinner and thinner! Your own son Peter . . . I've heard him moan in his sleep, he's so hungry! (*Crossing around L. end of table to below it.*) And you come in the night and steal food that should go to them . . . to the children!

MRS. VAN DAAN. He needs more food than the rest of us. He's used to more. He's a big man. (*Mr. Van Daan breaks away, moving up toward the mantel.*)

MRS. FRANK. (*Turning on Mrs. Van Daan.*) And you . . . you're worse than he is! You're a mother, and yet you sacrifice your child to this man! . . . this . . . this . . . ! (*She moves up* L. *of table, to above it.*)

MR. FRANK. (*Moving down to* L. *of her.*) Edith! Edith! (*Margot picks up the pink woolen stole from the chair* R. *of the table, putting it over Mrs. Frank's shoulders.*)

MRS. FRANK. (*Paying no attention, going on to Mrs. Van Daan.*) Don't think I haven't seen you! Always saving the choicest bits for him! I've watched you day after day and I've held my tongue. But not any longer! Not after this! Now I want him to go. I want him to get out of here. (*Moves* U. C. *Mr. Frank and Mr. Van Daan speak together.*)

MR. FRANK. Edith!   MR. VAN DAAN. Get out of
                                                      here?

MRS. VAN DAAN. What do you mean? (*Sinking into chair* R. *of table.*)

MRS. FRANK. Just that! Take your things and get out! (*Mr. Van Daan sits on upstage end of couch.*)

MR. FRANK. (*To Mrs. Frank.*) You're speaking in anger. You cannot mean what you are saying.

MRS. FRANK. I mean exactly that! (*Warn* W. C. *on.*)

MR. FRANK. For two long years we have lived here, side by side. We have respected each other's rights . . . we have managed to live in peace. Are we now going to throw it all away? (*Moving to above* R. *chair. Mr. Van Daan fears that he is going to retch.*) I know this will never happen again, will it, Mr. Van Daan?

MR. VAN DAAN. No. No. (*Holding his mouth and stomach, he starts for the* W. C. *Anne puts her arms around him, helping him up the steps. Mrs. Van Daan rises to help, but they have gone. She moves to the sofa, takes cover from the Franks' bed, puts it around her shoulders.*)

MRS. FRANK. He steals once! He'll steal again!

MR. FRANK. Edith, please! Let us be calm. We'll all go to our rooms . . . and afterwards we'll sit down quietly and talk this out . . . we'll find some way . . . (*W.* C. *on.*)

MRS. FRANK. No! No! No more talk! I want them to leave! (*Mr. Frank realizes he cannot reason with her. He makes a hopeless gesture and goes to Anne and Margot* U. R. C.)

MRS. VAN DAAN. (*Wandering* L. *below table.*) You'd put us out, on the streets?

MRS. FRANK. There are other hiding places.

MRS. VAN DAAN. A cellar . . . a closet. I know. And we have no money left even to pay for that.

MRS. FRANK. I'll give you money. Out of my own pocket I'll give it gladly. (*She gets her purse from the shelves* U. L. *and comes back with it to the center table. Mr. Frank crosses down to above* R. *end of table.*)

MRS. VAN DAAN. (*Comes to above chair* L. *of table.*) Mr. Frank, you told Putti you'd never forget what he'd done for you when you came to Amsterdam. You said you could never repay him, that you . . .

MRS. FRANK. (*Counting out money.*) If my husband had any obligation to you, he's paid it, over and over.

MR. FRANK. Edith, I've never seen you like this before. I don't know you.

MRS. FRANK. I should have spoken out long ago.

MR. DUSSEL. You can't be nice to some people.

MRS. VAN DAAN. (*To Mr. Dussel.*) There would have been plenty for all of us, if you hadn't come in here! (*Warn W. C. off.*)

MR. FRANK. We don't need the Nazis to destroy us. We're destroying ourselves. (*He sits down,* R. *of table, with his head in his hands. Mrs. Frank comes to Mrs. Van Daan with some money in her hands.*)

MRS. FRANK. Give this to Miep. She'll find you a place. (*She forces the money into Mrs. Van Daan's hand and returns her purse to* U. L. *shelves.*)

ANNE. (*W. C. off. Crossing to* U. L. C.) Mother, you're not putting Peter out. Peter hasn't done anything.

MRS. FRANK. (*Coming to Anne.*) He'll stay, of course. When I say the children, I mean Peter too. (*Peter rises from the steps where he has been sitting.*)

PETER. I'd have to go if Father goes. (*Mr. Van Daan comes from the bathroom. Mrs. Van Daan hurries to him and takes him to the couch, where he sits on upstage end. Then she goes to the sink to get water to bathe his face.*)

MRS. FRANK. (*To Peter, while this is going on, crossing down to above table.*) He's no father to you . . . that man! He doesn't know what it is to be a father.

PETER. (*Starting for his room.*) I wouldn't feel right I couldn't stay

MRS. FRANK. Very well then. I'm sorry. (*She crosses upstage again.*)

ANNE. (*Rushing over to Peter.*) No. Peter! No! (*Peter goes into his room, closing the door after him. He goes into his closet area. Anne turns back to her mother, crying.*) I don't care about the food. They can have mine! I don't want it! Only don't send them away. It'll be daylight soon. They'll be caught. . . .

MARGOT. Please, Mother!

MRS. FRANK. They're not going now. They'll stay here until Miep finds them a hiding place. (*Coming back to R. above the table, speaking to Mrs. Van Daan.*) But one thing I insist on! He must never come down here again! He must never come to this room where the food is stored! We'll divide what we have . . . an equal share for each! (*Mr. Dussel hurries over to get a sack of potatoes from the food safe. Mrs. Frank goes on, to Mrs. Van Daan.*) You can cook it here and take it up to him. (*She moves u. c. again. Mr. Dussel brings the sack of potatoes to the c. table.*)

MARGOT. (*Coming to L. of Mr. Dussel.*) Oh, no! No! We haven't sunk so far that we're going to fight over a handful of rotten potatoes.

MR. DUSSEL. (*Dividing the potatoes into piles.*) Mrs. Frank, Mr. Frank, Margot, Anne, Peter, Mrs. Van Daan, Mr. Van Daan, myself . . . Mrs. Frank . . . (*Buzzer. The buzzer sounds in Miep's signal. All freeze for an instant.*)

MR. FRANK. (*Rises quickly.*) It's Miep! (*He hurries over to his bed, snatches up his overcoat, and, putting it on, starts to the stairwell.*)

MARGOT. At this hour?

MRS. FRANK. (*Crossing to D. R. of the table, Mr. Van Daan rises, holds D. R.*) It must be trouble.

MR. FRANK. (*Turning back at head of stairwell to Mr. Dussel.*) I beg you, don't let her see a thing like this!

MR. DUSSEL. (*Who has been counting without stopping.*) Anne, Peter, Mrs. Van Daan, Mr. Van Daan, myself, Mrs. Frank . . .

MARGOT. (*To Mr. Dussel, overlapping.*) Stop it! Stop it!

MR. DUSSEL. . . . Mr. Frank, Margot, Anne, Peter, Mrs. Van Daan, Mr. Van Daan, myself, Mrs. Frank . . .

MRS. VAN DAAN. (*Pointing at the potato piles.*) You're keeping the big ones for yourself! All the big ones. . . . (*Coming down below table.*) Look at the size of that! . . . and that! . .

(Mr. Dussel continues on with his dividing. Peter, with his shirt and trousers on, comes from his room and stops just outside his door.)

MARGOT. *(To Mr. Dussel.)* Stop it! Stop it! *(We hear Miep's excited voice, speaking to Mr. Frank outside.)*

MIEP. Mr. Frank . . . the most wonderful news . . . the invasion has begun!

MR. FRANK. No! No!

MIEP. *(She comes running up the steps, ahead of Mr. Frank. She has a man's raincoat on over her nightclothes, and is carrying a bunch of flowers.)* Did you hear that, everybody? Did you hear what I said? The invasion has begun! *(They all stare at Miep, unable to grasp what she is telling them. Mr. Frank returns and holds at extreme D. L.)* The invasion! *(Peter is the first to recover his wits.)*

PETER. Where?

MIEP. It began early this morning! *(As she goes on, they crowd around her, listening tensely . . . all but Mr. Van Daan, who listens from R.)*

MRS. FRANK. *(To Miep.)* How do you know?

MIEP. The radio! . . . The B.B.C.! They said they landed on the coast of Normandy!

PETER. The British?

MIEP. British, Americans, French, Dutch, Poles, Norwegians . . . all of them! More than four thousand ships! *(As Miep goes on, the realization of what is happening begins to come to them. Everyone goes crazy with excitement.)* Churchill spoke, and General Eisenhower! D-Day they call it! *(A wild demonstration takes place. Peter rushes up to the kitchen, and grabs a frying pan. Anne follows him. He starts to march around the room, followed by Anne, and then by Margot. They circle the center table, singing the Dutch National Anthem. They dum-ta-dum the melody, not using the words. Miep gives Margot the bunch of flowers as Margot passes her. Peter pounds out the beat of the music on the frying pan. Peter and Anne end U. R., inspecting the map hanging above the mantel. Margot starts to distribute the flowers to everyone. During this the "grownups" embrace each other. All enmities are forgotten in the exhilaration of the wonderful news. Mrs. Frank hugs Mr. Van Daan, as Mr. Frank hugs Miep and Mrs. Van Daan.)*

MR. FRANK. Thank God it's come!

MRS. VAN DAAN. At last! (*Mrs. Frank turns from Mr. Van Daan to go to Miep and Mr. Frank. Only Mr. Van Daan does not join in the excitement. He is too ashamed of himself. Mrs. Frank meets Mrs. Van Daan D. C., as Mrs. Van Daan is going over to embrace Mr. Van Daan, D. R. The two women hug each other with warm affection. Then Mrs. Frank goes over, hugging Miep and Mr. Frank. Mrs. Van Daan gives Mr. Van Daan an ecstatic embrace, then starts up to Mr. Dussel, above the center table. Mr. Van Daan sits on the downstage end of the couch, too heartbroken to rejoice with the rest. As Mrs. Van Daan goes up to hug Mr. Dussel, Mrs. Frank has the same thought. The two women do a little dance of jubilation with Mr. Dussel. Then Mrs. Frank hurries D. L. as Miep starts for the door.*)

MIEP. (*At the stairwell.*) I'm going to tell Mr. Kraler. . . . This'll be better than any blood transfusion!

MR. FRANK. (*Stopping her.*) What part of Normandy did they land, did they say?

MIEP. Normandy . . . that's all I know now. I'll be up the minute I hear some more! (*She goes quickly out.*)

MR. FRANK. (*Taking Mrs. Frank in his arms.*) What did I tell you! What did I tell you! (*Mrs. Frank indicates that he has forgotten to bolt the door after Miep. He hurries down the steps. Margot goes down L. to give a flower to Mr. Van Daan. As she holds it out to him, he suddenly breaks into a convulsive sob. Mrs. Van Daan rushes to him. She sits on the couch, above, trying to comfort him. Margot, not understanding the outburst, retreats to C. below the table.*)

MRS. VAN DAAN. Putti! Putti! What is it? What happened?

MR. VAN DAAN. Please. I'm so ashamed. (*Mr. Frank comes back up the steps.*)

MR. DUSSEL. (*Impatient, coming down.*) Oh, for God's sake! (*He goes back to the table, putting the potatoes into the bag.*)

MRS. VAN DAAN. (*Comfortingly.*) Don't, Putti.

MARGOT. It doesn't matter now!

MR. FRANK. (*Going to Mr. Van Daan.*) Didn't you hear what Miep said? The invasion has come! We're going to be liberated! This is a time to celebrate! (*He hurries up to the cupboard and gets the cognac and a glass. He brings them to the table R. of Mr. Dussel, and pours a stiff drink.*)

MR. VAN DAAN. To steal bread from children.

92

MRS. FRANK. (*Below* L. *end of table.*) We've all done things that we're ashamed of.

ANNE. (*Coming down to him. To Mr. Van Daan.*) Look at me, the way I've treated Mother . . . so mean and horrid to her.

MRS. FRANK. No, Anneline, no. (*Anne goes to her mother, putting her arms around her.*)

ANNE. Oh, Mother, I was. I was awful.

MR. VAN DAAN. Not like me! No one is as bad as me!

MR. DUSSEL. (*Bag of potatoes under his arm, flower in hand, he has circled* L. *of the table and crosses to* D. R. C. *Speaks to Mr. Van Daan.*) Stop it now! Let's be happy!

MR. FRANK. (*Giving Mr. Van Daan the glass of cognac.*) Here! Here! Schnapps! Locheim! (*Mr. Van Daan takes the cognac. They all watch him. Anne crosses to Mr. Van Daan and puts up her fingers in a V-for-Victory sign. As Mr. Van Daan gives a faint smile and an answering V-sign, they are startled to hear a loud wailing sob from behind them. They all look over. It is Mrs. Frank, stricken with remorse. She has sunk quietly into the* D. L. *chair. Crossing to her.*) Edith . . . !

MRS. FRANK. (*Mr. Frank crosses to* L. *of her, patting her hand. Anne and Margot rush across, kneel at her feet to comfort her. Mrs. Van Daan remains on the couch. Through her sobs.*) When I think of the terrible things I said . . .

MR. VAN DAAN. (*Earnestly, as he crosses to her, holding out the glass of cognac and making a V-sign.*) No! No! You were right!

MRS. FRANK. (*Still sobbing.*) That I should speak that way to you . . . our friends . . . our guests . . .

MR. DUSSEL. Stop it! You're spoiling the whole invasion! (*Dim fast drop in. Work light on. Curtain light on. As Mr. Dussel says "spoiling," the scene lights dim out quickly, leaving the group in a lag special. This special fades swiftly and the black drop is brought in.*)

ANNE'S VOICE. (*Faintly at first and then with growing strength.*) We're all in much better spirits these days. There's still excellent news of the invasion. The best part about it is that I have a feeling that friends are coming. Who knows? Maybe I'll be back in school by Fall. Ha, ha! The joke is on us! The warehouse man doesn't know a thing and we are paying him all that money! Wednesday, the second of July, nineteen forty-four. The invasion seems temporarily to be bogged down. Mr. Kraler has to have an operation,

93

which looks bad. The Gestapo have found the radio that was stolen. Mr. Dussel says they'll trace it back and back to the thief, and then it's just a matter of time 'til they get to us. Everyone is low. Even poor Pim can't raise their spirits. I have often been downcast myself . . . but never in despair. I can shake off everything if I write. But . . . and that is the great question . . . (*Work light off.*) will I ever be able to write well? I want to so much. (*Black drop out. Work light off. Drop out. Dim up slow.*) I want to go on living even after my death. (*Lights begin slow fade up. Voice begins to fade out.*) Another birthday has gone by, so now I am fifteen. Already I know what I want. I have a goal, an opinion. (*Voice out. Lights three-quarters full and rising.*)

ACT II

SCENE 4

It is an afternoon a few weeks later.
Everyone but Margot is in the Center room. There is a sense of great tension. In the distance a German military band is heard in a rendition of some Viennese waltzes. (Sound Cue 30.) Mr. Dussel is standing at the window up C., *looking down fixedly at the street below. Margot is at the dressing table in the Right room. The table lamp is on. Peter is sitting* R. *of the center table, with his copy books, trying to do his lessons. Anne sits* R. *of the table, writing in her diary. Mrs. Van Daan is seated on the couch, a book beside her, her eyes on Mr. Frank, as he sits in the* D. L. *chair. Mrs. Frank is* U. C. *pacing, looking fearfully toward the stairwell. As the lights fade up. Mr. Van Daan is pacing from* D. C. *to* R. *He reverses and goes to Mr. Frank. There is no reaction from Mr. Frank, so he starts* R. *again and is* D. R. C. *when the telephone in the office below begins to ring. Phone. Mr. Van Daan turns around, looking toward the stairwell. Mrs. Frank stops, tight with fear. They are all rigid, listening tensely. The telephone continues to ring throughout the scene. Mr. Dussel rushes down* L. *of the table to Mr. Frank.*

94

MR. DUSSEL. There it goes again, the telephone! Mr. Frank, do you hear?

MR. FRANK. (*Quietly.*) Yes. I hear.

MR. DUSSEL. (*Pleading, insistent.*) But this is the third time, Mr. Frank! The third time in quick succession! It's a signal! I tell you it's Miep, trying to get us! For some reason she can't come to us and she's trying to warn us of something!

MR. FRANK. Please. Please.

MR. VAN DAAN. (*To Mr. Dussel, as he goes up to* R. *above table.*) You're wasting your breath.

MR. DUSSEL. Something has happened, Mr. Frank. For three days now Miep hasn't been to see us! And today not a man has come to work. There hasn't been a sound in the building!

MRS. FRANK. (L. C. *above table.*) Perhaps it's Sunday. We may have lost track of the days.

MR. VAN DAAN. (*To Anne.*) You with the diary there. What day is it? (*Anne closes the diary so he cannot read what she is writing.*)

MR. DUSSEL. (*Coming up to Mrs. Frank.*) I don't lose track of the days! I know exactly what day it is! It's Friday, the fourth of August. Friday, and not a man at work! (*He rushes down to Mr. Frank again, pleading with him, almost in tears.*) I tell you Mr. Kraler's dead. That's the only explanation. He's dead and they've closed down the building, and Miep's trying to tell us!

MR. FRANK. She'd never telephone us.

MR. DUSSEL. (*Frantic, indicating ringing telephone.*) Mr. Frank, answer that! I beg you, answer it!

MR. FRANK. No.

MR. VAN DAAN. (*Hurrying around the* R. *end of the table and crossing to Mr. Frank.*) Just pick it up and listen. You don't have to speak. Just listen and see if it's Miep.

MR. DUSSEL. For God's sake . . . I ask you.

MR. FRANK. (*Firmly.*) No. I've told you no. I'll do nothing that might let anyone know we're in the building.

PETER. Mr. Frank's right.

MR. VAN DAAN. (*Wheeling on his son.*) There's no need to tell us what side you're on!

MR. FRANK. If we wait patiently, quietly, I believe that help will come. (*There is silence for a minute as they all listen to the telephone ringing. Mr. Dussel moves up to* L. *Mr. Van Daan circles* R. *of the table to above it.)*

MR. DUSSEL. I'm going down. *(He rushes down the steps. Mr. Frank tries ineffectually to stop him. Mrs. Frank also makes a lunge to stop him but fails. When Mr. Dussel reaches the door outside the telephone stops. Site—Phone stops. He rushes out anyway. Mr. Frank waits tensely, wondering if he should go after Mr. Dussel. Mrs. Frank moves upstage of the stairwell, gazing down tensely. Peter rises. After a long moment Mr. Dussel returns, shuts the door and comes up the stairs.)* Too late. *(Mr. Frank crosses above the table and enters the Right room. He looks out the edge of the blackout curtain, then goes to Margot. Mr. Dussel returns to his* U. C. *window. Mrs. Frank goes to the sink, gets potatoes and sits on the padded stool above the stove, peeling them.)*

MR. VAN DAAN. (U. C.) So we just wait here until we die.

MRS. VAN DAAN. *(Hysterically.)* I can't stand it! I'll kill myself! I'll kill myself!

MR. VAN DAAN. *(Coming to* L. *below table.)* For God's sake, stop it!

MRS. VAN DAAN. I think you'd be glad if I did! I think you want me to die!

MR. VAN DAAN. Whose fault is it we're here? *(Crossing to her. She covers her ears.)* We could've been safe somewhere . . . in America or Switzerland. *(She rises, starts toward the stairs* U. L. *He follows, shouting.)* But no! No! You wouldn't leave when I wanted to! You couldn't leave your things! You couldn't leave your precious furniture! *(He grabs her arm as she starts up the stairs. She shakes him off.)*

MRS. VAN DAAN. Don't touch me! *(Mrs. Van Daan goes quickly upstairs. Mr. Van Daan follows slowly after her. Peter, humiliated, desperate, goes to his room. Anne looks after him, deeply concerned. Peter throws himself face down on his cot. Mr. Dussel goes back to his post at the window and Mrs. Van Daan lies sobbing quietly on her bed. Mr. Frank comes out into the Center room, goes down to the couch and picks up the book lying there. He sits on the couch trying to read. Anne rises and quietly goes to Peter's room, closing the door after her. She sits on the edge of the cot and leans over him, holding him in her arms, try-*

ing to bring him out of his despair. Peter is too unhappy to re-
spond. After a second Anne starts to talk to him.)

ANNE. (*Looking up through skylight.*) Look, Peter, the sky. What
a lovely day. Aren't the clouds beautiful? You know what I do
when it seems as if I couldn't stand being cooped up for one more
minute? I think myself out. I think myself on a walk in the park
where I used to go with Pim. Where the daffodils and the crocus
and the violets grow down the slopes. You know the most wonderful thing about *thinking* yourself out? You can have it any
way you like. You can have roses and violets and chrysanthemums
all blooming at the same time. . . . It's funny . . . I used to take
it all for granted . . . and now I've gone crazy about everything
to do with nature. Haven't you?

PETER. (*Barely lifting his face.*) I've just gone crazy. I think if
something doesn't happen soon . . . if we don't get out of here
. . . I can't stand much more of it! (*Warn change. Curtain light
on. Warn £54.*)

ANNE. (*Softly.*) I wish you had a religion, Peter.

PETER. (*Bitterly, as he rolls over.*) No, thanks. Not me.

ANNE. Oh, I don't mean you have to be Orthodox . . . or believe in heaven and hell and purgatory and things. . . . I just
mean some religion . . . it doesn't matter what. Just to believe in
something! When I think of all that's out there . . . the trees . . .
and flowers . . . and seagulls . . . when I think of the dearness
of you, Peter . . . and the goodness of the people we know . . .
Mr. Kraler, Miep, Dirk, the vegetable man, all risking their lives
for us every day. . . . When I think of these good things, I'm
not afraid any more. . . . I find myself, and God, and I . . .

PETER. (*Impatiently, as he gets to his feet.*) That's fine! But when
I begin to think, I get mad! Look at us, hiding out for two years.
Not able to move! Caught here like . . . waiting for them to come
and get us . . . and all for what?

ANNE. (*Rises and goes to him.*) We're not the only people that've
had to suffer. There've always been people that've had to . . .
sometimes one race . . . sometimes another . . . and yet . . .

PETER. (*Sitting on upstage end of bed.*) That doesn't make me
feel any better!

ANNE. I know it's terrible, trying to have any faith . . . when
people are doing such horrible . . . (*Gently lifting his face.*)
but you know what I sometimes think? I think the world may be

going through a phase, the way I was with Mother. It'll pass, maybe not for hundreds of years, but some day. . . . I still believe, in spite of everything, that people are really good at heart.

PETER. (*Rising, going to the windowseat.*) I want to see something now. . . . Not a thousand years from now.

ANNE. (*As she comes to him.*) But, Peter, if you'd only look at it as part of a great pattern . . . that we're just a little minute in life. . . . (*She breaks off.*) Listen to us, going at each other like a couple of stupid grownups! (*She holds out her hand to him. He takes it.*) Look at the sky now. Isn't it lovely? (*Site [as Peter puts his hands on Anne's shoulders.] Peter rises, stands behind her with arms around her. They look out at the sky.*) Some day, when we're outside again I'm going to . . . (*She breaks off as she hears the sound of a car outside, its brakes squealing as it comes to a sudden stop, [Sound Cue 31.] The people in the other rooms also become aware of the sound. They listen tensely. Another car outside roars up to a sudden stop. [Sound Cue 31 concluded.] Mr. Frank, book in hand, rises slowly. Everyone is listening, hardly breathing. Suddenly a heavy electric bell begins clanging savagely below. [Sound Cue 32.] Anne and Peter hurry from the Left room. She stops just outside the door. He remains on the first step. Mr. Dussel comes to u. c. Margot hurries into the room. Mrs. Frank puts down the potatoes and comes to above chair R. of c. table. Mrs. Van Daan comes down the stairs fearfully. Mr. Van Daan stays above at head of staircase. All eyes are fixed on Mr. Frank. He crosses slowly, calmly, toward the stairwell. He drops book on D. L. chair. The bell stops. [Sound Cue 32 ends.] Mr. Frank turns to the others, makes a reassuring gesture, then starts down the stairwell. The bell begins another long peal. [Sound Cue 33.] Mr. Dussel comes down and follows Mr. Frank out. Peter follows after Mr. Dussel. The bell stops. [Sound Cue 33 ends.] Watching them go, Mrs. Frank moves to R. of the c. table. Margot comes down, taking Mrs. Frank's hand. Mrs. Van Daan crosses to u. c. Mr. Van Daan comes down the stairs to L. of her. There is a motionless silence, then Mr. Dussel re-enters, coming up the stairs with Peter close behind. The bell starts clanging again. [Sound Cue 34.] As Mr. Dussel gets a step into the room, he slumps to his knees. Peter helps him to his feet. Shaking off Peter's help, Mr. Dussel crosses below to his room, enters and starts packing. The bell stops. [Sound Cue 34 ends.] From far below, we hear a door being bat-*)

tered down. [Sound Cue 35.] Mr. Frank returns, bolting the door behind him. The door below crashes. There is the sound of booted footsteps, [Sound Cue 36.] then another door is battered through. [Sound Cue 37.] They all look to Mr. Frank as he stops at the head of the stairwell. He makes a gesture that tells all. A moan escapes Mrs. Van Daan and she sags. Peter and Mr. Van Daan go to her, helping her to the padded stool U. R. Mrs. Frank sinks down in the chair R. of the C. table, resting her head forward on the table top. Margot clings to the back of the chair. Mr. Frank moves quickly toward the shelves U. L., then stops U. L. C. and turns to speak to the others.)

MR. FRANK. For the past two years we have lived in fear. Now we can live in hope. (Cellar light off. Mr. Frank picks up a leatherette shopping bag and Anne's school bag from under the shelves. Moving quickly he gives the school bag to Anne, who has remained just outside Peter's open door. The other he gives to Margot and in pantomime asks her where Mrs. Frank's bag is. Margot indicates the W. C. He goes to get it. As Mr. Frank finishes his last speech a pair of boots clump heavily up a flight of stairs to the office below. [Sound Cue 38.] They sound very near. On 3rd rifle blow dim med. slow. Count 1-2-3-4. Lag out. Drop in. Work light on. Curtain light on. Mr. Van Daan starts upstairs to pack. Peter comes to Anne, kissing her good-bye. Then, crossing behind her, he goes into his room to pack. Margot crosses U. L. to collect her things. As Peter crossed to Anne the door buzzer sounded. A short pause, then another insistent buzz. Mr. Frank re-enters after Peter has gone and gives a bag to Mrs. Frank. He stands R. of her, holding her hand. She raises her head. After the second buzz, a rifle butt crashes heavily into their bolted door below. [Sound Cue 39.] With greater and greater violence the blows fall. Shouted commands are heard.)

MEN'S VOICES. Auf machen! Da drinnen! Auf machen! Schnell! Schnell! Schnell! etc., etc. (Mr. and Mrs. Frank look over at Anne. She stands, holding her school satchel, looking back at them with a soft, reassuring smile. She is no longer a child, but a woman with courage to meet whatever lies ahead. The lights begin to dim on the third stroke. Scene lights are out by the seventh stroke, leaving Anne in a lag special. The lag fades out by the ninth blow and we hear a mighty crash as the door is shattered. The black drop is brought in. After a second Anne's Voice is heard.)

ANNE'S VOICE. And so it seems our stay here is over. They are waiting for us now. They've allowed us five minutes to get our things. We can each take a bag and whatever it will hold of clothing. Nothing else. So, dear Diary, that means I must leave you behind. Good-bye for a while. P.S. Please, please, Miep, or Mr. Kraler, or anyone else. If you should find this diary will you please keep it safe for me, because some day I hope . . . (*When ready work light off. Drop out. Dim up—slow. Her voice stops abruptly. There is silence. After a second the CURTAIN RISES.*)

ACT II

Scene 5

It is again the afternoon in November, 1945. The rooms are as we saw them in the first scene. (Sound Cue No. 2 without the clock can be repeated here.)
Mr. Kraler has joined Miep and Mr. Frank. The center table has been put upright. Coffee cups are on it for Mr. Kraler and Miep. He sits below the table on the padded stool, she is R. of the table, sitting on a straight backed chair. Mr. Frank is seated on the couch. The lamp table has been pulled out to the upstage end of the couch and the lamp replaced on it. Its shade is missing. Mr. Frank's coffee cup is on the lamp table. The black drop rises on a dark stage. The naked bulb in the lamp begins to glow and the scene lights fade up slowly around this lead. When full, we can see it is early evening. The lighting is cool, save the small area around the naked bulb. We see a great change in Mr. Frank. He is calm now. His bitterness is gone. He slowly turns a few pages of the diary. They are blank. Warn curtain. Warn house Lights.

MR. FRANK. No more. (*He closes the diary and puts it on the couch beside him.*)
MIEP. I'd gone to the country to find food. . . . When I got back the block was surrounded by police. . . .
MR. KRALER. We made it our business to learn how they knew.

It was the thief . . . the thief who told them. (*Mr. Kraler indicates to Miep that she should refill the cups. She starts to the gas burner for the coffee pot.*)

MR. FRANK. (*After a pause, quietly, simply.*) It seems strange to say this, that anyone could be happy in a concentration camp. But Anne was happy in the camp in Holland where they first took us. After two years of being shut up in these rooms, she could be out . . . out in the sunshine and the fresh air that she loved.

MIEP. (*She has come down with the pot.*) A little more?

MR. FRANK. (*He doesn't really hear her. After a beat he realizes what she has said.*) Yes, thank you. (*She pours his coffee. He continues his story as she pours for Mr. Kraler and for herself, and returns pot to stove. Then she sits at the table again.*) The news of the war was good. The British and Americans were sweeping through France. We felt sure that they would get to us in time. In September we were told that we were to be shipped to Poland . . . the men to one camp. The women to another. I was sent to Auschwitz. They went to Belsen. In January we were freed, the few of us who were left. The war wasn't yet over, so it took us a long time to get home. We'd be sent here and there behind the lines where we'd be safe. Each time our train would stop . . . at a siding, or a crossing . . . we'd all get out and go from group to group. . . . Where were you? Were you at Belsen? At Buchenwald? At Mathausen? Is it possible that you knew my wife? Did you ever see my husband? My son? My daughter? That's how I found out about my wife's death . . . of Margot, the Van Daans, Peter . . . Dussel. But Anne . . . I still hoped. (*He picks up the diary.*) Yesterday I went to Rotterdam. I'd heard of a woman there. She'd been in Belsen with Anne. . . . I know now. (*He opens the diary and turns the pages back to find a certain passage. As he finds it, we hear Anne's Voice. His eye falls on a sentence.*)

ANNE'S VOICE. In spite of everything, I still believe that people are really good at heart.

MR. FRANK. She puts me to shame. (*Dim med. slow. Curtain. Work light on. The lights begin to fade. Mr. Frank slowly closes the diary. The lights are out.*)

THE CURTAIN FALLS

"THE DIARY OF ANNE FRANK"

"HANUKKAH"

YIDDISH FOLK SONG

ALLEGRO

OH HAN-UK-KAH OH HAN-UK-KAH THE SWEET CEL-E-BRA-TION A-

-ROUND THE FEAST WE GATH-ER IN COM-PLETE JUB-IL-A-TION

HAP-PI-EST OF SEA-SONS NOW IS_ HERE MAN-Y ARE THE REASONS

FOR GOOD CHEER TO-GETH-ER WE'LL WEATH-ER WHAT EV-ER TO-MOR-ROW MAY

BRING SO HEAR US RE-JOIC-ING AND MER-RI-LY VOIC-ING THE

(SHOUT)

HAN-UK-KAH SONG THAT WE SING HEY! SO HEAR US RE-JOIC-ING AND

MER-RI-LY VOIC-ING THE HAN-UK-KAH SONG THAT WE SING.

DUTCH NATIONAL ANTHEM

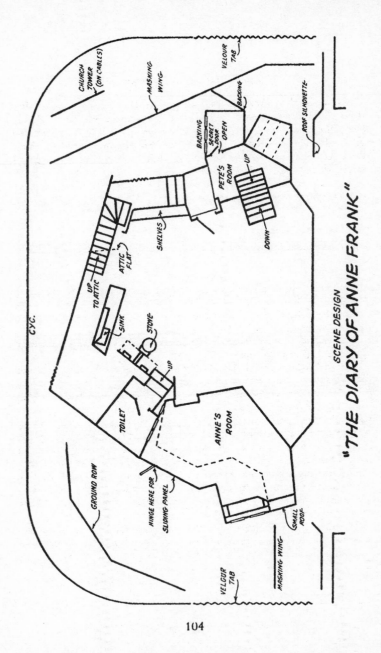

SCENE DESIGN

"THE DIARY OF ANNE FRANK"

PRODUCTION NOTES

It is possible to eliminate the platform in the Center room, leaving Anne's and Peter's rooms on platforms. Hers about one foot high, his about three feet six inches. The stairs going down can be eliminated by making a tunnel under Peter's room. This tunnel should be about three feet high by two feet six inches wide, with a door opening onstage. All enter on hands and knees.

It is also possible to eliminate the Attic room if necessary, and have the stairs lead to a platform off L.

GENERAL NOTES

Although each of the acts is divided into 5 scenes, there should be a flow, making the act seem like one scene. This is accomplished by cross-fading lights and the sound at the beginning and end of each scene. The one exception to this method is between II-4 and II-5—there are several seconds of deliberate silence in the blackout after "some day I hope ——" The black drop for scene changes should not be seen coming in or going out.

The bag of potatoes used by Mr. Dussel in II-3 are baked for easy handling and to avoid their rolling around.

A signal light is rigged for all entrances from the basement, if a trap door is used.

Since four prop men and four dressers are on the stage for the changes, bringing the total people on the set to 16, a system is used whereby each actor on the blackout, always goes to one spot on the set for his change. Anne goes to her room. Mr. Dussel goes to the W. C. Mr. Frank goes to the head of the basement stairs; after I-1 and II-4 he goes to the basement landing. Mrs. Frank goes to the area behind the stove and sink. Peter goes to his room. Mr. and Mrs. Van Daan to the attic or to the foot of the stairs leading to the attic. Margot goes to the area by the shelves behind the curtains up L. C. Each prop man and dresser has time for only one trip on and off.

In order to give the impression that they have lost weight, in the second act, Mr. and Mrs. Frank and Mr. and Mrs. Van Daan wear clothing similar to theirs of Act I but in a larger size.

KEY TO PRONUNCIATIONS

AMEN	OH-MEIN
AMSTERDAM	AHM'-STER-DAHM
ANNE	AH'-NAH or the familiar AH'-NEE
ANNEKE	AH'-NAH-KAH
ANNELINE	AH'-NAH-LYNN
AUSCHWITZ	AOW''-SHVITZ
BELSEN	BELL'-SEN
BUCHENWALD	BUCH'-EN-VALD
DELPHI	DELL'-FIE
DIRK	DEE'-URK
DUSSEL	DUSS'-ELL
EDITH	AE'-DIT
FRANK	FRAHNK
HALLENSTEINS	HA'-LEN-STAINS
HILVERSUM	HILL'-VER-SUM
JAN	YAN
JOPIE	YO'-PEE
KERLI	CARE'-LEE
KRALER	KRAH'-LER
LIEFJE	LEAF'-YAH
MARGOT	MAR'-GOTT
MAUTHAUSEN	MAUT'-HOW-SEN
MAZELTOV	MAH'-ZEL-TAHV
MIEP	MEEP
MOUSCHI	MOO'-SHE
OTTO	AH'-TOE
PETER	PAY'-TER
PETRONELLA	PET-ROW-NELL'-AH
PUTTI	POO'-TEE
ROTTERDAM	RAH'-TER-DAHM
VAN DAAN	FAHN DAHN
WESSELS	VESS'-ELLS
WESTERTOREN	VESS'-TER-TOR-EN
WILHELMINA	VIL-HEL-MEE'-NAH

PROPERTY PLOT

Act I—Scene 1

Center Room (See drawing)

Table c. upset
High-back chair to R. of table upset
High-back chair up L. upset
Oval chair down L. upset
Round table above sofa
Stool above round table
Round chair above stairwell
Tattered drape pulled onstage up L.
Drape up R. drawn to conceal sink
Tear piece on sofa
Sheet in sofa pull-out half, also pillow
Glove on floor by round table
Scarf hanging upstage of door L.
Old curtain on window up c.
Bed roll concealed under stairs up L.
Stove in front of mantel
Pin-flags for war map on mantel
Lamp on mantel
Sink, running water—dish cloth hanging on water pipe
2-burner gas plate
Dish towel hung on leg of gas plate
Empty saucepan on stove
On sink: Empty coffee pot, cup and saucer, glass, mixing bowl, wooden spoon
On shelf over sink: 5 glasses, paring knife, boxes of safety matches, lid, kettle, canister of flour
Dish pan hanging to L. of sink
Under sink: 2 pieces of dark bread, bag of baked potatoes, bag of beans, bucket to catch waste water, dummy grocery parcels
Hanging above sink: Skillet, funnel, pot, ladle
On shelves up L.: Top shelf: Small wash-tub for cat. Electric iron, 8 glasses, cognac bottle filled with tea, flashlight, practical, deck of cards, chess set, pile of linens, spare dish cloth, spare crossword book, 9 cups and saucers, 8 bread and butter plates, mirror, 8 napkins, 8 napkin rings, 8 knives and forks, cake knife, cigarette box with 2

cigarettes and box of matches, packet of papers, letters, notes, Anne's diary, old one, 20 bottles assorted medicines, 4 large bars of white soap, table cloth

Carpet beater hanging by shelves

Table lamp concealed behind sofa

Blue knitting on round chair above stair well

Kettle on back of stove in front of mantel

Room L. (Peter's):

Mattress on door supported by two boxes

Bed made up: Ticking, sheet, blanket, ticking cover

Pictures on wall

Concealed in orange crate: Bottle of orange juice, capped, bottle opener, 2 glasses, cup of water, comb, mirror, shoe brush, wood for carving, pencils in small brown jug, crossword book, towel

Concealed on floor: Pillow, 10 books, dictionary, saucer

On shelf: Dead plant, student lamp

Blackout curtain at base of skylight

Empty rucksack hanging behind curtains that conceal escape

Attic

Bed made up with sheet and blanket

Orange crate

Box used as stool

Chair with back removed

Barrel

Cigarette machine

Deck of cards

Needlepoint frame, yarn and needle

Nasal atomizer

3 paper-wrapped parcels

Cloth for cleaning fur coat

Mirror, light, and box in dressing area off attic

Newspaper

Room Right (Anne's)

Sofa, with sheet and blanket attached and concealed

Bed, made up with ticking, sheet, blanket and ticking cover

Small cabinette under bed

Blackout curtains in place over window

10 books in window box

Pair of socks on window seat

Sewing basket on small box shelf containing: Needle and thread, over-sized brassiere, measuring tape, Kleenex, pair of white gloves (spare)

Chest of drawers against rear wall and below window
On top: 3 books, scissors
In top drawer: Pillow for bed
In bottom drawer: Comb and brush (spare), pair of white gloves (spare)
Round low stool at foot of sofa
Low cut-off box to complete length of sofa for sleeping. (Contains speaker used for Anne's voice in I-1)
Iron washstand-dresser
On top: Oval mirror, lying face down, small manicure set
On shelf: Book, hair ribbon, newspaper
Under: Large cabinette, containing spare newspaper
On floor by washstand, lamp concealed
Check:
Blackout of work lights
Creak effect in place
Reading light for bridge by microphone off L.
Water running
All doors closed except one to Peter's room ⅔ open
Off U. R.:
Cat in carrier and leash
Small plant
Hat box
Paper wrapped parcel
Two blankets and one pillow for the bed-sofa in Center room
Small straw carry-all

Basement—Act J

Straw shopping bag, containing comb, hair brush and pairs of stockings (Miep)
Pill bottles, satchel and briefcase stuffed (Kraler)
Red shopping bag stuffed (Mrs. Frank)
Plaid school satchel stuffed (Anne)
Grocery bag with thermos of milk and several newspaper-wrapped parcels (Margot)
Pocket watch and chain; fountain pen filled; shoe box containing clippings of movie stars, photo of Queen Wilhelmina, and a new diary (Mr. Frank)
Briefcase stuffed, leather shopping bag stuffed, small medicine kit filled with bottles, extra pill bottles (Mr. Dussel)
Briefcase containing quart of milk (dummy), 2 real cabbages, and loaf of bread (Mr. Kraler)

1—2 Strike:
Rip on sofa
Rucksack and diary
Blue knitting
Ticking on Peter's bed
Pictures in Peter's room
Dead plant
Ticking on bed in Anne's room
Set lamps—on rd. table s. R., dressing table—Anne's room
Move torn curtain
Move mixing bowl to shelf
Set up furniture: Armchair to R. of table, straight to L. of table
1—3:
Clear table (c.)
Set:
Pipe—shelf on rd. table—s. R.
Knitting on sofa
Glass of fake milk on sink
Beans and pot on sink
Map above fireplace
2 composition books and 2 pencils (c. table)
Bread basket behind stove
Lesson book and 2 pencils and 2 shopping lists on Anne's dresser
Apron near sink
Move upstage straight chair to c. of table
Strike thermos bottle
1—4—Set:
Pink shawl on chair R. of c. table
Blanket on bed
Fix sofa for sleeping
Fix bed roll
Move stool above stove
Clear mantel
Clear c. table
1—5—Set: Water pitcher, cookies, nuts, prayer book, table cloth,
  Menorah, wine, fruit, 2 boxes of matches
(All placed on c. table and rd. table AFTER they are moved into place
  in front of sofa)
Set:
Hat lampshade on dresser in Anne's room
Satchel with gifts beside Anne's dresser
Satchel contains:
  1. Wrapped used crossword book tagged with poem
  2. Bottle of homemade shampoo wrapped in paper

3. 2 homemade cigarettes in large box
4. Envelope containing IOU
5. Poorly made knitted muffler
6. Ball of paper wrapped in red ribbon
7. Used safety razor
8. 2 capsules in small box

Strike:

Lampshade on dresser in Anne's room
Move lamp (table R.) behind sofa
Move C. table and round table in front of sofa
Move sofa upstage on marks
Make up Anne's and Mr. Dussel's beds
Put bed roll away

BETWEEN ACTS

Strike:

Table setting, menorah, candles and gifts
Reset furniture with armchair D. L.

Set:

Clothes line
Book—chair D. L.
Diary and pen on C. table
(Fur coat in attic pre-set)
Hanukkah scarf on sofa
Blanket on sofa
Teapot filled on sink
8 cups on sink (moved from shelves)
Anne's room—pair of frayed pants and scissors on dresser
Anne's room—manicure set on dresser
Pink shawl on sofa
Papers on Anne's dresser (top and bottom)
Purse and money on 3rd shelf U. L.
Apron near sink (or is being worn by Mrs. Frank)
Empty all luggage and reset

Basement—Act II

Cake on a plate, inscribed "Peace in 1944" (1 layer·chocolate icing, white decoration, 6" diameter)
Bunch of fake flowers tied together (Asters)
Several books
Shopping bag containing newspaper-wrapped parcels of food
Newspaper-wrapped box of candy—fake
Bunch of loose carnations (10)

II—2—Set:

Photos in Peter's room

Magazine on c. table
Ledger, paper and pencil on c. table
Glove and needle on chair D. L.
4 books under mirror in Anne's room
Replace comb and brush on Anne's dresser
Move pink shawl from sofa to dresser in Anne's room
Move stool D. S. of table
Move scarf to hook U. L.
Strike:
Cake and cake plates (scattered)
Blanket on sofa
Book in chair D. L.
Papers on floor in Anne's room
JJ—3—Strike:
Ledger and pink material
4 books under mirror—Anne's dresser
Clear c. table
Move stool to stove
Move pink shawl on chair R. of table (C.)
Make up sofa for sleeping
Make bed roll for sleeping
Cup and saucer and glass on sink
JJ—4—Set:
Rd. chair to sink
Pot, potatoes and knife and plate to sink
Pad, pencil, diary and pen to c. table
Book and 2 pillows on sofa
Fix bed in Anne's room
Close sofa
Clear bed roll
Move stool D. S. of c. table
Clear table
Check rucksack and shopping bag in W. C.
Change plant in Peter's room
JJ—5—Strike:
Bedding and clothes and curtain in Anne's room into window seat
Ticking on Peter's bed
Kettle and pot on stove
On:
Tray—3 cups and saucers; sugar and creamer and coffee pot
Rip to sofa
Move shade from lamp on rd. table behind sofa
Change to dead plant in Peter's room

COSTUME PLOT

Otto Frank

I—1:

Pink shirt, black tie, trousers, vest, old brown overcoat, scarf attached,
shoes, stockings. During scene on scarf

I—2:

Off: Overcoat, muffler. During scene off: Hat, overcoat, shoes.
On: Hat, jacket with star, new overcoat with star

I—3:

Off: Jacket without star. During scene on shoes
On: Grey sweater

I—4:

Off: Sweater, vest, shoes. During scene on new overcoat (star removed)
On: Pajamas, slippers

I—5:

Off: Overcoat, pajamas. During scene off: Hat
On: Jacket without star, hat

II—1:

Brown shirt, blue tie, large trousers, large vest with watch and chain,
sweater, black loafers

II—2:

Off: Sweater, loafers
On: Tweed jacket, slippers

II—3:

Off: Tweed jacket, vest. During scene on: Overcoat
On: Pajamas

II—4:

Off: Overcoat, pajamas, slippers
On: Tweed jacket, loafers

II—5:

Off: Tweed jacket
On: Old overcoat, scarf attached

Anne Frank

I—2:

Beret, pink blouse with star, gray skirt, cape with star, gloves, 4 panties,
red sweater with star, white sweater, gray stockings, shoes. During
scene off: Gloves, sweaters, cape, 3 panties, shoes, star from blouse

113

J—3:

On: Red sweater. During scene on: Shoes, hair bow. During scene on and off: Peter's cap, Peter's trousers, Peter's jacket, Mrs. Van Daan's fur coat without star

J—4:

Off: Bow, blouse, skirt, shoes, stockings, red sweater
On: Nightgown

J—5:

Off: Nightgown
On: Red dress, beige stockings, shoes

II—1: Slip, yellow sweater, green skirt, shoes (no stockings)

II—2:

Off: Skirt, sweater. During scene on: Blue blouse, blue skirt, white gloves, pink shawl, Margot's shoes

II—3:

Off: Shawl, blouse, gloves, shoes. During scene on: Green skirt used as a make-shift cape
On: Nightgown, blue sweater

II—4:

Off: Nightgown
On: Shoes

MRS. FRANK

J—2:

Blouse, jabot, skirt and jacket, red sweater, nightgown over above, overcoat with star over all. Carried: Bag, hat, gloves, shoes, grey stockings. During scene off: Jacket, jabot, nightgown, overcoat, sweater

J—3:

Off: Shoes. During scene on: Shoes, apron

J—4:

Off: Blouse, skirt, shoes, apron
On: Green dress, nightgown. During scene on and off: Pink shawl

J—5:

Off· Nightgown. During scene off: Shoes
On: Shoes, lace shawl, earrings and necklace

II—1:

Worn large blouse, worn large skirt, worn large jacket, small jabot, gloves with fingers cut off. During scene off: Gloves

II—2:

Off: Jacket, jabot

II—3:

Off: Shoes, blouse
On: Nightgown. During scene on: Pink shawl

II—*4*:
Off: Nightgown
On: Pink blouse, shoes

MARGOT FRANK

I—*2*:
Yellow shirt, green skirt, yellow sweater, pink nightgown, purple skirt, gray cotton stockings (worn through play), shoes, coat with star, green hat, gloves and belt in pocket of coat. During scene off: Hat, gloves, coat, purple skirt, nightgown, yellow sweater, shoes
I—*3*:
Roll up sleeves on shirt. During scene on: Shoes, apron
I—*4*:
Off: Apron, shoes, shirt, skirt. On: Nightgown, slippers. During scene on: Robe. During scene off: Robe (behind curtain), nightgown, slippers. During scene on: Pink Jersey top, purple skirt, earrings, shoes
I—*5*:
As end of I—4. During scene off: Shoes
II—*1*:
Purple skirt, lavender shirt, sleeves rolled, wine shirt, yellow sweater, Mrs. Frank's red sweater, pink stole, scarf
II—*2*:
Off: Stole, scarf, red sweater. On: Special shoes for Anne. During scene off: Special shoes. During scene on: Slippers
II—*3*:
Off: Yellow sweater, wine skirt. On: Nightgown. During scene on: Robe
II—*4*:
Off: Robe, nightgown, slippers. On: Shoes

MR. VAN DAAN

I—*2*:
Padding, undershirt, shirt and tie, trousers with suspenders, jacket with star, shoes, stockings, vest, overcoat with star, gloves, hat. Underdressed: Shirt and tie. Concealed between vest and jacket: Shirt and sweater. During scene off: Overcoat, hat, gloves, shoes, vest, shirt, sweater, jacket. During scene on: Jacket
I—*3*:
Remove: Star from jacket. On: Shoes
I—*4*:
Off: Jacket, shirt and tie, shoes
I—*5*:
On: Shirt and tie, jacket with handkerchief in pocket, vest, shoes, hat. During scene off: Hat

II—1:
Off: Padding, large shirt, large trousers, sweater, gloves, slippers
II—2:
Off: Sweater
II—3:
Off: Shirt, slippers
II—4:
On: Shirt, jacket

Mrs. Van Daan
I—2:
Blouse, skirt, jacket, fur coat with star, hat, gloves, bag, shoes, stockings, bed jacket, apron. During scene off: Apron, bed jacket, fur coat, gloves
I—3:
Off: Jacket, shoes. On: Jabot. During scene on: Shoes
I—4:
Off: Shoes. On: Nightgown, slippers. During scene off: Slippers, nightgown, jabot, blouse, skirt. During scene on: Gold evening dress
I—5:
As end of I—4. During scene off: Shoes
II—1:
Large blouse, large skirt, slippers, Peter's raincoat, scarf
II—2:
Off: Raincoat, scarf. During scene on: Apron
II—3:
Off: Apron. On: Nightgown. During scene on: Blanket from sofa as makeshift cape
II—4:
Off: Nightgown. On: Jacket, apron

Peter Van Daan
I—2:
Black shoes, brown stockings, pajama trousers, new trousers, belt, old trousers tied around waist, brown knickers, new blue shirt, bow tie, new blue sweater with star, vest with star, new jacket with star, rain coat, cap. During scene off: Vest, jacket, raincoat, jacket, star from sweater, old trousers
I—3:
Off: Knickers, shoes, sweater. During scene on: Shoes
I—4:
Off: Tie, shoes, trousers. On: Robe, slippers
I—5:
Off: Robe, slippers. On: Trousers, shoes, blue tie, vest, old jacket, cap. During scene off: Cap, shoes

II—1:

Black shoes, brown stockings, old trousers, belt, pajama trousers, padding, old blue shirt, tie, old sweater. old jacket, wool cap

II—2:

Off: Jacket, tie, sweater. On: Red tie, vest, jacket

II—3:

Off: Tie, vest, trousers, shirt, padding. During scene on: Shirt, trousers, slippers

II—4:

Off: Shirt. On: Sweater

Dussel

(Preset in W. C.—Jacket, quick-change tie, dentist coat without star, green sweater, slippers)

I—3:

Sweat shirt, pajamas, handkerchief in breast pocket, black shoes, stockings, new gray shirt, tie, new pants, dentist's coat with star, trench coat, hat, glasses, wrist watch

I—4:

Strip to pajamas (dresser takes everything to W. C. to preset for I—5)

I—5:

Jacket, quick tie, shirt, shoes, stockings, glasses. (After I—5, set jacket in Dussel's room, set shoes in W. C., take 1st act dentist's coat and tie to dressing room)

II—1:

Old shirt, tie, old trousers, glasses, slippers, stockings, Mr. Frank's overcoat

II—2:

Off: Overcoat, slippers. On: Dentist's coat without star, shoes

II—3:

Off: Shoes, dentist's coat. On: Slippers, pajamas. During scene on: Jacket, glasses

II—4:

Off: Pajamas, jacket. On: Green sweater

Miep

I—1:

Underdressed: Blue skirt, 2 sweaters, collar. Purple skirt, baby padding, hat, shoes, gray stockings, crucifix, shorty coat

I—2:

Off: Coat, skirt, padding, hat

II—1:

Scarf, long coat, green skirt, green blouse, hat, gloves

117

𝕴𝕴—3:
Off: Scarf, long coat, green skirt, green blouse, hat, gloves. On: Night-gown, scarf, Dirk's raincoat (Dussel wears in I—3)
𝕴𝕴—5:
Same as I—1, not underdressed, plus matron's blouse

MR. KRALER

𝕴—2:
Brown jacket, vest, shirt, tie, trousers, shoes, stockings, hearing aid
𝕴—3:
Change tie
𝕴𝕴—1:
Change tie. On: Overcoat
𝕴𝕴—5:
Carry hat

LIGHT CUES

Act I—Scene 1
1—Dim up to opening
2—Trap sneak out
3—Dim out I—1
Act I—Scene 2
4—Dim up I—2
5—Bump on Anne bracket
6—Bump out Anne bracket
7—Dim out I—2
Act I—Scene 3
8—Dim up I—3
81—W. C. on
82—Anne lamp out
83—W. C. out
84—Anne lamp on
85—Attic on
86—Attic off
9—Anne bracket on
10—Dim out I—3
Act I—Scene 4
11—Dim up I—4
12—Anne bracket on
13—Center lamp on
14—Peter's lamp on
15—Attic on
16—Center table lamp on
16A—W. C. on
17—Peter's light off
18—Center lamp off
19—Attic off
21—Center table lamp off
—Bump off Anne bracket, then
22—Dim out I—4
Act I—Scene 5
23—Dim up I—5
27—Mantel lamp off

28—Center lamp off
29—Mantel lamp on
30—Slight dim for candle blow-out
31—Dim out I—5
Act II—Scene 1
40—Dim up II—1
—Sneak out LAG
40A—W. C. on
41—Anne bracket on
42—Dim out II—1
Act II—Scene 2
43—Dim up II—2
43A—Anne bracket off
43B—Down c.
—W. C. on
—W. C. off
—W. C. on
44—Up c., down Peter
45—Dim out II—2
Act II—Scene 3
48—Dim up II—3
50—On c. lamp
—W. C. on
—W. C. off
—Sneak up lag
51—Dim out II—3

Act II—Scene 4
52—Dim up II—4
54—Up c., down Peter
55—Dim out II—4

Act II—Scene 5
56—Dim up II—5
57—Dim out II—5

(Rail only used with Curtain calls.)

SOUND EFFECTS

Carillon and ships' whistles
Clock strikes 6
Children playing
Street organ
Ships' whistles
Quarter hour chimes
Marching feet
Children playing and singing
Carillon melody — then clock strikes 8 o'clock
Street and canal sounds
Car coming to stop, pause, then starts away
Bombers overhead
Streetcar
Marching men
Drunken soldiers singing "Lili Marlene"
Girl's high giggle
Footsteps on cobblestones
Sound of heavy boots
Planes high overhead
Streetcar passing
Dog barking
Feet running downstairs
Carillon chimes (hymn)
German band
Children playing, whistles in distance
Clock strikes 9 o'clock — melody first
Harbor whistles
German band playing Viennese waltzes
Car coming to a stop — then another
Heavy electric bell clanging
Electric bell — long peal
3rd clang from electric bell
Door being battered down
Boots run upstairs
Second door being battered through
Boots clump upstairs
Blows from rifle butt crashing into door, shouted commands

NEW PLAYS

★ **THE EXONERATED by Jessica Blank and Erik Jensen.** Six interwoven stories paint a picture of an American criminal justice system gone horribly wrong and six brave souls who persevered to survive it. "The #1 play of the year...intense and deeply affecting..." *–NY Times.* "Riveting. Simple, honest storytelling that demands reflection." *–A.P.* "Artful and moving...pays tribute to the resilience of human hearts and minds." *–Variety.* "Stark...riveting...cunningly orchestrated." *–The New Yorker.* "Hard-hitting, powerful, and socially relevant." *–Hollywood Reporter.* [7M, 3W] ISBN: 0-8222-1946-8

★ **STRING FEVER by Jacquelyn Reingold.** Lily juggles the big issues: turning forty, artificial insemination and the elusive scientific Theory of Everything in this Off-Broadway comedy hit. "Applies the elusive rules of string theory to the conundrums of one woman's love life. Think *Sex and the City* meets *Copenhagen.*" *–NY Times.* "A funny offbeat and touching look at relationships...an appealing romantic comedy populated by oddball characters." *–NY Daily News.* "Where kooky, zany, and madcap meet...whimsically winsome." *–NY Magazine.* "STRING FEVER will have audience members happily stringing along." *–TheaterMania.com.* "Reingold's language is surprising, inventive, and unique." *–nytheatre.com.* "...[a] whimsical comic voice." *–Time Out.* [3M, 3W (doubling)] ISBN: 0-8222-1952-2

★ **DEBBIE DOES DALLAS adapted by Erica Schmidt, composed by Andrew Sherman, conceived by Susan L. Schwartz.** A modern morality tale told as a comic musical of tragic proportions as the classic film is brought to the stage. "A scream! A saucy, tongue-in-cheek romp." *–The New Yorker.* "Hilarious! DEBBIE manages to have it all: beauty, brains and a great sense of humor!" *–Time Out.* "Shamelessly silly, shrewdly self-aware and proud of being naughty. Great fun!" *–NY Times.* "Racy and raucous, a lighthearted, fast-paced thoroughly engaging and hilarious send-up." *–NY Daily News.* [3M, 5W] ISBN: 0-8222-1955-7

★ **THE MYSTERY PLAYS by Roberto Aguirre-Sacasa.** Two interrelated one acts, loosely based on the tradition of the medieval mystery plays. "... stylish, spine-tingling...Mr. Aguirre-Sacasa uses standard tricks of horror stories, borrowing liberally from masters like Kafka, Lovecraft, Hitchcock...But his mastery of the genre is his own...irresistible." *–NY Times.* "Undaunted by the special-effects limitations of theatre, playwright and *Marvel* comic-book writer Roberto Aguirre-Sacasa maps out some creepy twilight zones in THE MYSTERY PLAYS, an engaging, related pair of one acts...The theatre may rarely deliver shocks equivalent to, say, *Dawn of the Dead*, but Aguirre-Sacasa's work is fine compensation." *–Time Out.* [4M, 2W] ISBN: 0-8222-2038-5

★ **THE JOURNALS OF MIHAIL SEBASTIAN by David Auburn.** This epic one-man play spans eight tumultuous years and opens a uniquely personal window on the Romanian Holocaust and the Second World War. "Powerful." *–NY Times.* "[THE JOURNALS OF MIHAIL SEBASTIAN] allows us to glimpse the idiosyncratic effects of that awful history on one intelligent, pragmatic, recognizably real man..." *–NY Newsday.* [3M, 5W] ISBN: 0-8222-2006-7

★ **LIVING OUT by Lisa Loomer.** The story of the complicated relationship between a Salvadoran nanny and the Anglo lawyer she works for. "A stellar new play. Searingly funny." *–The New Yorker.* "Both generous and merciless, equally enjoyable and disturbing." *–NY Newsday.* "A bitingly funny new comedy. The plight of working mothers is explored from two pointedly contrasting perspectives in this sympathetic, sensitive new play." *–Variety.* [2M, 6W] ISBN: 0-8222-1994-8

DRAMATISTS PLAY SERVICE, INC.
440 Park Avenue South, New York, NY 10016   212-683-8960   Fax 212-213-1539
postmaster@dramatists.com   www.dramatists.com

NEW PLAYS

★ **MATCH by Stephen Belber.** Mike and Lisa Davis interview a dancer and choreographer about his life, but it is soon evident that their agenda will either ruin or inspire them—and definitely change their lives forever. "Prolific laughs and ear-to-ear smiles." *–NY Magazine.* "Uproariously funny, deeply moving, enthralling theater. Stephen Belber's MATCH has great beauty and tenderness, and abounds in wit." *–NY Daily News.* "Three and a half out of four stars." *–USA Today.* "A theatrical steeplechase that leads straight from outrageous bitchery to unadorned, heartfelt emotion." *–Wall Street Journal.* [2M, 1W] ISBN: 0-8222-2020-2

★ **HANK WILLIAMS: LOST HIGHWAY by Randal Myler and Mark Harelik.** The story of the beloved and volatile country-music legend Hank Williams, featuring twenty-five of his most unforgettable songs. "[LOST HIGHWAY has] the exhilarating feeling of Williams on stage in a particular place on a particular night...serves up classic country with the edges raw and the energy hot...By the end of the play, you've traveled on a profound emotional journey: LOST HIGHWAY transports its audience and communicates the inspiring message of the beauty and richness of Williams' songs...forceful, clear-eyed, moving, impressive." *–Rolling Stone.* "...honors a very particular musical talent with care and energy... smart, sweet, poignant." *–NY Times.* [7M, 3W] ISBN: 0-8222-1985-9

★ **THE STORY by Tracey Scott Wilson.** An ambitious black newspaper reporter goes against her editor to investigate a murder and finds the *best* story...but at what cost? "A singular new voice...deeply emotional, deeply intellectual, and deeply musical..." *–The New Yorker.* "...a conscientious and absorbing new drama..." *–NY Times.* "...a riveting, tough-minded drama about race, reporting and the truth..." *–A.P.* "... a stylish, attention-holding script that ends on a chilling note that will leave viewers with much to talk about." *–Curtain Up.* [2M, 7W (doubling, flexible casting)] ISBN: 0-8222-1998-0

★ **OUR LADY OF 121st STREET by Stephen Adly Guirgis.** The body of Sister Rose, beloved Harlem nun, has been stolen, reuniting a group of life-challenged childhood friends who square off as they wait for her return. "A scorching and dark new comedy... Mr. Guirgis has one of the finest imaginations for dialogue to come along in years." *–NY Times.* "Stephen Guirgis may be the best playwright in America under forty." *–NY Magazine.* [8M, 4W] ISBN: 0-8222-1965-4

★ **HOLLYWOOD ARMS by Carrie Hamilton and Carol Burnett.** The coming-of-age story of a dreamer who manages to escape her bleak life and follow her romantic ambitions to stardom. Based on Carol Burnett's bestselling autobiography, *One More Time.* "...pure theatre and pure entertainment..." *–Talkin' Broadway.* "...a warm, fuzzy evening of theatre." *–BrodwayBeat.com.* "...chuckles and smiles of recognition or surprise flow naturally...a remarkable slice of life." *–TheatreScene.net.* [5M, 5W, 1 girl] ISBN: 0-8222-1959-X

★ **INVENTING VAN GOGH by Steven Dietz.** A haunting and hallucinatory drama about the making of art, the obsession to create and the fine line that separates truth from myth. "Like a van Gogh painting, Dietz's story is a gorgeous example of excess—one that remakes reality with broad, well-chosen brush strokes. At evening's end, we're left with the author's resounding opinions on art and artifice, and provoked by his constant query into which is greater: van Gogh's art or his violent myth." *–Phoenix New Times.* "Dietz's writing is never simple. It is always brilliant. Shaded, compressed, direct, lucid—he frames his subject with a remarkable understanding of painting as a physical experience." *–Tucson Citizen.* [4M, 1W] ISBN: 0-8222-1954-9

DRAMATISTS PLAY SERVICE, INC.
440 Park Avenue South, New York, NY 10016 212-683-8960 Fax 212-213-1539
postmaster@dramatists.com www.dramatists.com

NEW PLAYS

★ **INTIMATE APPAREL by Lynn Nottage.** The moving and lyrical story of a turn-of-the-century black seamstress whose gifted hands and sewing machine are the tools she uses to fashion her dreams from the whole cloth of her life's experiences. "…Nottage's play has a delicacy and eloquence that seem absolutely right for the time she is depicting…" *–NY Daily News.* "…thoughtful, affecting…The play offers poignant commentary on an era when the cut and color of one's dress—and of course, skin—determined whom one could and could not marry, sleep with, even talk to in public." *–Variety.* [2M, 4W] ISBN: 0-8222-2009-1

★ **BROOKLYN BOY by Donald Margulies.** A witty and insightful look at what happens to a writer when his novel hits the bestseller list. "The characters are beautifully drawn, the dialogue sparkles…" *–nytheatre.com.* "Few playwrights have the mastery to smartly investigate so much through a laugh-out-loud comedy that combines the vintage subject matter of successful writer-returning-to-ethnic-roots with the familiar mid-life crisis." *–Show Business Weekly.* [4M, 3W] ISBN: 0-8222-2074-1

★ **CROWNS by Regina Taylor.** Hats become a springboard for an exploration of black history and identity in this celebratory musical play. "Taylor pulls off a Hat Trick: She scores thrice, turning CROWNS into an artful amalgamation of oral history, fashion show, and musical theater…" *–TheatreMania.com.* "…wholly theatrical…Ms. Taylor has created a show that seems to arise out of spontaneous combustion, as if a bevy of department-store customers simultaneously decided to stage a revival meeting in the changing room." *–NY Times.* [1M, 6W (2 musicians)] ISBN: 0-8222-1963-8

★ **EXITS AND ENTRANCES by Athol Fugard.** The story of a relationship between a young playwright on the threshold of his career and an aging actor who has reached the end of his. "[Fugard] can say more with a single line than most playwrights convey in an entire script…Paraphrasing the title, it's safe to say this drama, making its memorable entrance into our consciousness, is unlikely to exit as long as a theater exists for exceptional work." *–Variety.* "A thought-provoking, elegant and engrossing new play…" *–Hollywood Reporter.* [2M] ISBN: 0-8222-2041-5

★ **BUG by Tracy Letts.** A thriller featuring a pair of star-crossed lovers in an Oklahoma City motel facing a bug invasion, paranoia, conspiracy theories and twisted psychological motives. "…obscenely exciting…top-flight craftsmanship. Buckle up and brace yourself…" *–NY Times.* "…[a] thoroughly outrageous and thoroughly entertaining play…the possibility of enemies, real and imagined, to squash has never been more theatrical." *–A.P.* [3M, 2W] ISBN: 0-8222-2016-4

★ **THOM PAIN (BASED ON NOTHING) by Will Eno.** An ordinary man muses on childhood, yearning, disappointment and loss, as he draws the audience into his last-ditch plea for empathy and enlightenment. "It's one of those treasured nights in the theater—treasured nights anywhere, for that matter—that can leave you both breathless with exhilaration and…in a puddle of tears." *–NY Times.* "Eno's words…are familiar, but proffered in a way that is constantly contradictory to our expectations. Beckett is certainly among his literary ancestors." *–nytheatre.com.* [1M] ISBN: 0-8222-2076-8

★ **THE LONG CHRISTMAS RIDE HOME by Paula Vogel.** Past, present and future collide on a snowy Christmas Eve for a troubled family of five. "…[a] lovely and hauntingly original family drama…a work that breathes so much life into the theater." *–Time Out.* "…[a] delicate visual feast…" *–NY Times.* "…brutal and lovely…the overall effect is magical." *–NY Newsday.* [3M, 3W] ISBN: 0-8222-2003-2

DRAMATISTS PLAY SERVICE, INC.
440 Park Avenue South, New York, NY 10016 212-683-8960 Fax 212-213-1539
postmaster@dramatists.com www.dramatists.com